M

THE GRANDLUXE EXPRESS

RAILROADS PAST AND PRESENT

George M. Smerk, editor

THE
GRAND LUXE
EXPRESS
Traveling in High Style

KARL ZIMMERMANN

INDIANA UNIVERSITY PRESS

Bloomington and Indianapolis

This book is a publication of

Indiana University Press
601 North Morton Street
Bloomington, IN 47404-3797 USA

http://iupress.indiana.edu

Telephone orders   800-842-6796
Fax orders   812-855-7931
Orders by e-mail   iuporder@indiana.edu

The paper used in this publication meets the
minimum requirements of American National
Standard for Information Sciences—Permanence
of Paper for Printed Library Materials,
ANSI Z39.48-1984.

Manufactured in China

Library of Congress Cataloging-in-Publication Data

Zimmermann, Karl R.
  The GrandLuxe Express : traveling in high style /
Karl Zimmermann.
     p. cm. — (Railroads past and present)
  Includes bibliographical references.
  ISBN-13: 978-0-253-34947-7 (cloth : alk. paper)
1. GrandLuxe Express (Express train) 2. American
Orient Express (Express train)—History. 3. Railroad cars—
United States—History. I. Title.
  TF25.G73Z56 2007
  385.0973—dc22

                              2007015144

1 2 3 4 5 12 11 10 09 08 07

FACING PAGE: The *American Orient Express* westbound on ex–Denver & Rio Grand
Western rails near Tunnel #1 at Clay, Colorado. *Steve Patterson.*

PREVIOUS PAGES: In August 1996, the 16-car-long *American Orient Express* rolls
eastbound at Rollins, Colorado. *Joe McMillan.*

FOLLOWING PAGES: The *American Orient Express* crosses the Utah Desert.
Karl Zimmermann.

For Laurel, who has made the journey so much finer

CONTENTS

ACKNOWLEDGMENTS IX

Introduction: Cruising on the *GrandLuxe Express* 1

1. Ancestry 11

2. The *American-European Express* Comes and Goes 29

3. *American Orient Express:* The Phoenix Rises 55

4. The Old Order Changeth: GrandLuxe Rail Journeys 81

5. Silk Purses: GrandLuxe's Glamorous Cars 105

6. Life on Board 125

APPENDIX 141
BIBLIOGRAPHY 145

The *New York* observation glows cozily during a service stop at Klamath Falls, Oregon. *Bob Johnston.*

ACKNOWLEDGMENTS

My long acquaintance with the *GrandLuxe Express* and its predecessors has led to encounters with many wonderful individuals, both crew and passengers, each of whom has helped shape my sense of the train. My experience with this unique enterprise dates to November of 1989, when I traveled from Washington to New York on the *American-European Express.* In October of 1997 I made my first journey on the *American Orient Express,* and I've ridden the train at least once a year since then, as study leader for Smithsonian Associates, host for the Society of International Railway Travelers, or on-board lecturer.

Of the personnel on the train, the tour leaders are no doubt the people I remember best. I won't attempt to list them all for fear of omission, but I will mention Megan Harvist, now the on-board tour manager, with whom I've traveled often and who has been particularly helpful with and supportive of this project. In the *American Orient Express* offices, Kathleen Cusack was unfailingly collaborative and congenial over many years. Though I never met her, I came to consider her a friend.

Greg Mueller I *have* now met, though he had been an invaluable source of information about the train and encouraged my interest in it for many years before that. He worked for the *American-European Express,* was president for a time of the *American Orient Express,* and is now vice-chairman of GrandLuxe Rail Journeys; thus he has a literally unique perspective on the history of the company. Greg has been enormously generous with his time and unfailingly gracious in answering my endless questions. The book as it now exists would have been literally impossible without him—a friend for sure.

John Kirkwood also has a long history with the train. Cars of his Rail Ventures company were part of the operation from the very beginning, and some remain in the consist today. In addition, he served for years on the *AOE* board of directors. He too was unstinting in sharing his time and insights.

When Colorado Railcar entered the picture to provide this book's figurative if not literal final chapter, it suddenly became essential that I get a clear view of both Tom Rader's background and his vision for GrandLuxe Rail Journeys, the company that he was suddenly leading. In our many hours of conversation, he could not have been more helpful and forthcoming, always taking whatever time was needed to answer my myriad questions.

Photography obviously is hugely important to a book like this one, and here again I've had splendid allies. Steve Patterson, Joe McMillan, Jim Shaughnessy, Chip Sherman, Bruce C. Nelson, Bob Johnston, Alex Mayes, Bob Turner, and Ralcon Wagner all contributed photographs. Peter V. Tilp provided both his own photography and some from his collection; Dave Randall opened his collection, as did Richard Stoving.

Though Roger Cook's photographic contribution to this book is more limited than typically, everything I write and think about railroads has been informed and shaped by our 50 years of friendship in trains. Rich Taylor, another friend, has cheerfully run down some elusive facts when I couldn't.

Small sections of the text that follows first appeared in different form in *Trains, Classic Trains, Passenger Train Journal,* and *Locomotive & Railway Preservation.* My thanks to the editors of those publications for rewarding collaborative experiences over the years.

As always, no one deserves more thanks than my wife, Laurel, my frequent traveling companion, sounding board, tireless editor, and gentle critic.

THE GRANDLUXE EXPRESS

In Denver, lounge car *Rocky Mountain* is swathed in snow and ice from a freak October snowstorm in 1997. *Karl Zimmermann.*

The chargers are out for dinner on the *American Orient Express*.
Karl Zimmermann.

Porters welcome passengers back
to the *American Orient Express*.
Karl Zimmermann.

FACING PAGE: Luncheon aboard *AOE*'s
former Union Pacific dining-room
car *Jasper. Karl Zimmermann.*

Introduction
CRUISING ON THE *GRANDLUXE EXPRESS*

Picture this. You're sitting on the circular settee in a bullet-shaped, deep-windowed observation car named *New York,* listening to the rumble of wheels on rail and watching the steep, rocky walls of the Colorado River's canyons sweep by. Inside, this historic car is all plush upholstery, wood accents, and stylish appurtenances. Outside, the scenery soars, some of the best in America.

As the afternoon wanes and the canyon's colors deepen into dusk, your fellow passengers aboard the *GrandLuxe Express* turn their attention to cocktails, mixed by the steward behind the commodious bar at the car's center. The hours ahead promise a fine five-course dinner in one of the train's two single-level dining cars or in the upper level of the dome car, also set for the evening meal: perhaps pistachio-encrusted goat cheese served with a sweet chili sauce; a roasted asparagus soup garnished with asparagus tips; a baby spinach salad with brie, bacon, and toasted pecans, finished with a poppy-seed vinaigrette; pan-seared duck breast with a wild rice pilaf and sautéed baby carrots, with a citrus ginger reduction; and blackberry shortcake with chantilly cream and blackberry liqueur sauce.

To understand what GrandLuxe Rail Journeys is all about, think luxury cruise ship—but on rails. That captures the essence of the *GrandLuxe Express,* a train that since 1994 has roamed North America (until May of 2006 under the name *American Orient Express*) offering itineraries ranging in length from four to ten nights. Days are divided between time aboard, as the train speeds or dawdles across the landscape, and time off the train on motor-coach tours, of either local attractions or grander ones such as our national parks.

Though the tours are central to travel aboard *GrandLuxe,* it's the train itself that makes the experience unique. And lovely indeed is the train. It was actually "trains," plural, for a few years, since from the fall of 2002 through the 2004 season there were two of them, *AOE I* and *AOE II,* also known as the Blue Train and the Red Train. And two trains there will most probably be again, since the current owners are planning a second trainset, this one bi-level.

For now, however, the train is a single, impressively long "consist," or combination of cars—as many as 21, all elegantly tricked out in blue, cream, and gold. These cars are classic, smooth-sided American light-weights on the outside, while inside they quite successfully evoke European Wagons-Lits *luxe.* If "American Orient Express" was an oxymoron, it nonetheless accurately defined the train's style and ambiance.

The cars that now form the *GrandLuxe Express* began life in the forties, fifties, and sixties as workaday sleepers, diners, lounges, and chair cars for such railroads as Union Pacific, Southern Pacific, and Chesapeake & Ohio. The one car that was most special from the outset brings up the rear of the train. It's the observation-lounge car *New York,* which was New York Central's *Sandy Creek*—the feature car of the world-renowned *20th Century Limited.* Full-length dome cars *Copper Canyon* and *New Orleans*—one of which is typically in the consist—have some claim to fame as well, having been feature cars on Great Northern's *Empire Builder.*

In 1989, a group of Swiss and American investors created the core of today's train by transforming ten (and one that came later) mostly plain-vanilla streamlined cars into the *American-European Express,* in effective emulation of Europe's famous (but by then vanished) *Orient Express.* With two consists of a diner, a lounge, and three sleepers, the train began by offering six-day-a-week service between Washington, D.C., and Chicago. Eventually a New York–Chicago option was added, and then all the cars (including the eleventh, the *New York*) combined as the *AEE*'s *Greenbrier Limited.* Within two years, however, the *American-European Express* had failed, but in 1994 the phoenix-like train began a new life as the *American Orient Express.* Since then, the train has grown, changed operators three times, and evolved to the peripatetic enterprise it is today.

In addition to the *New York* at the rear of the train and the dome in mid-consist, there are piano lounge cars mid-train, *Seattle* and *Rocky Mountain,* filled with overstuffed lounge chairs and settees. At each car's center is a baby grand piano, and at one end an ebony bar with an intertwined *AEE* logo (for the sharp-eyed, a surviving clue to the train's history). A pianist is always present in one of the lounges during cocktails and after dinner, and conviviality is very much the order of the evening.

The train's dining cars, *Chicago* and *Zurich,* are perhaps even more elegant than the piano lounges, with handsome wood paneling and marquetry. Dinner is served here and also in the dome. Wherever, the presentation is stylish indeed, featuring crisp white linen, china badged with the GrandLuxe logo, and fine glassware.

Beyond the good food, the elegance, the service, the tours, the camaraderie among passengers, and the trackside scenery, there's an ineffable something about just being on a train that accounts for the *AOE*'s and now *GrandLuxe*'s continuing popularity. It's part nostalgia, certainly, though you'd have to go back a long way to find the level of railbound luxury purveyed by *GrandLuxe*. Perhaps Edna St. Vincent Millay said it most famously, in her poem "Travel": "Yet there isn't a train I wouldn't take, / No matter where it's going."

Not that the train now operated by GrandLuxe Rail Journeys has encountered no bumps in the road. In the 18 years since the launch of the *American-European Express* in 1989, any number of luxury trains have started up with great fanfare. Almost all (including the *AEE*) have failed, and the *AOE*, too, struggled at times. Its classic cars were, by definition, also old cars, prone to the mechanical problems (particularly with air conditioning) that age brings. *AOE* suffered a serious derailment, as did *AEE* before it. Since the mid 1990s, freight railroads have merged and become significantly busier. This increased pressure on track capacity has made them often inhospitable hosts—either shunning the *AOE* completely or saddling it with hopelessly inconsistent timekeeping. While it might have seemed a simple matter to operate the *AOE* wherever there were adequately maintained rails, this was far from the truth. Track capacity and traffic density, locations suitable for secure overnight parking and servicing, and endless other factors often got in the way.

Getting *AOE II* on the rails proved to be no easy task, either. Additional equipment had to be found, acquired by lease or purchase, and refurbished to the standard of luxury set by the original train. Only one of the three tail cars that served opposite the *New York* in the two-plus seasons of *AOE II*'s operation came even close to being an adequate running mate, and the twin-unit diner purchased for the second train just didn't have the elegance of the pair originally created for *AEE*. Not surprisingly, this process of expansion resulted in start-up delays, and also in some cars being rushed prematurely into service.

There has been an ebb and flow of itineraries, with some falling by the wayside for lack of patronage or the unwillingness of freight railroads, on whose tracks the *AOE* would have run, to host. The development of new routes remains a complex task, typically taking well over a year. In addition, ongoing itineraries have been repeatedly tweaked—to make them better, but also out of operational necessity or for cost savings.

If the *GrandLuxe Express* is akin to a cruise ship, it may also seem a bit like the Flying Dutchman's ill-starred vessel, fated to roam the seven seas of North America for long periods without making it to home port. GrandLuxe Rail's shop facilities are located in Fort Lupton, Colorado (*AOE*'s were in Tenino, Washington, and before that Englewood, Colorado). If major mechanical problems crop up en route, the train is at the mercy of the local shops belonging to Amtrak or one of the host freight railroads, which, happily, have generally served it well.

Through it all, the *American Orient Express* kept on running, though it may well never have made a profit. The baton then passed to Grand-Luxe Rail Journeys, which is now writing the next chapter of this luxury train's interesting and convoluted story.

"Cruise train" is a term that has been bandied about for many decades. As the original *California Zephyr* fought for life in the sixties, the concept was invoked—not for the first time, no doubt, though the *CZ* was touted as the first train scheduled explicitly to traverse its route's finest scenery in daylight. But not until the *American Orient Express* became firmly established in the later 1990s did the cruise-train concept reach maturity. This posh, nomadic train largely abandoned the transportation function that originally was passenger railroading's raison d'etre. "Getting there is half the fun," the famous Cunard Line boast, could have been applied with accuracy to the *CZ*. Aboard the *Grand-Luxe Express,* as aboard the vast fleet of cruise ships that is active today, getting there is *all* the fun.

AOE's New York observation car rolls south near Palmer Lake,
Colorado, under a stormy August sky. *Joe McMillan.*

Dinnertime in the *Copper Canyon* dome car. *Karl Zimmermann.*

In October of 1997, the eastbound *AOE* encounters snow
in Colorado's Gore Canyon. *Karl Zimmermann.*

The westbound *AOE* exits Tunnel #1
in the Front Range of the Rockies.
Steve Patterson.

ABOVE: The "Pacific Coast Explorer" drops down into San Luis Obispo from Cuesta Pass on the former Southern Pacific. *Karl Zimmermann.*

LEFT: In Williams, Arizona, on a rainy morning. *Karl Zimmermann.*

FACING PAGE: Behind a streamlined J3 Hudson styled (like the rest of this 1938 train) by Henry Dreyfuss, the *20th Century Limited* has just raced under the Bear Mountain Bridge on its trip north along the Hudson River from New York City. *The Edward L. May Memorial Collection, courtesy Richard Stoving.*

1

Ancestry

To find the true roots of the *GrandLuxe Express,* for a dozen years called the *American Orient Express,* you have to look on both sides of the Atlantic.

Of the countless hundreds of elegant, often opulent passenger trains that have run on North American rails over the last century and a half, of all those expresses and limiteds, which train might be dubbed the truest ancestor of the *GrandLuxe Express*? The New York Central's New York City–Chicago *20th Century Limited,* perhaps America's most famous train ever, would be in the running, and some might argue for its greatest competitor, the Pennsylvania Railroad's *Broadway Limited.* Both were all-Pullman trains, surely a prerequisite. All-Pullman too were, among others, Illinois Central's Chicago–New Orleans *Panama Limited* and Atchison, Topeka & Santa Fe's Chicago–Los Angeles *Chief* and *Super Chief.*

This last is a strong candidate, certainly. The *Super Chief* had cachet to burn, and a passenger list peppered with movie stars and moguls. It was a quintessentially elegant and exclusive train, with "sailings" initially just once a week from Chicago and Los Angeles. Though a stand-in version with heavyweight equipment had inaugurated the name "Super Chief" the year before, the train's most exquisite incarnation came with the first lightweight or streamlined version of 1937. Built by the Edward G. Budd Manufacturing Company (later called The Budd Company) using its patented Shotwelding process to create peerless cars of its signature fluted stainless steel, this paragon was among the earliest full-size streamliners, with arguably the most stylish interiors ever created for a lightweight train.

Designers Paul Phillipe Cret and John Harbeson did the work for Budd, and their influences were Art Deco and the aesthetics, honestly expressed, of the Indians of the Southwest. Like the *GrandLuxe Express*'s cars, these were wood-paneled, but with a difference: Flexwood Veneer. This thin layer of real wood, mounted on muslin backing applied over masonite siding, allowed the designers to array the train with such rare and beautiful woods as Bubinga, white harewood, macassar ebony, ribbon primavera, zebrawood, Brazilian rosewood, ebonized maple, American holly, redwood burl, teak, aspen, and satinwood.

Service was superb, and the meals as well, under the aegis of the Fred Harvey Company, which for many decades made the Santa Fe's diners among the finest on rails. For the 1937 *Super Chief,* Santa Fe/Fred Harvey architect and designer Mary Jane Colter created a unique china pattern, which was used throughout the train's career. For her china, called "Mimbreño," Colter borrowed pictographs from the ancient Mimbres Indians, a different one for each dish. The *Super Chief* was one of the few trains ever to have its own proprietary china pattern; *American-European Express, American Orient Express,* and now *GrandLuxe Express* are others.

An even more apt place to look for *GrandLuxe* heritage might be a short-lived *Super Chief* ancestor on the same route: the *Santa Fe de Luxe.* This posh little train was inaugurated in December 1911 and lasted through 1918 as a weekly winter-season-only service with a six-car consist: diner, club car (with smoking room, barber shop, and shower), a 10-section observation parlor car, and three additional Pullmans: two all-drawing rooms and one all-compartment. This preponderance of private rooms over open sections (uppers and lowers, hung with curtains for privacy) was unusual in that era. Even the quintessentially luxurious *20th Century Limited* still offered mostly sections. And only the most elite trains had showers.

The *de Luxe* could accommodate just 60 passengers—at an extra fare of $25, a whopping surcharge for the time. The train's generous ratio of public space to sleeping accommodations was echoed in the *American-European Express* (which initially could accommodate just 56 passengers), and in GrandLuxe's current train, which carries 11 sleeping cars and 6 dining and lounge cars.

The *Santa Fe de Luxe* shamelessly flaunted its snob appeal. Its ads, including one featuring a snooty butler in tailcoat, proudly proclaimed "extra fare twenty-five dollars" rather than downplaying the surcharge. This princely sum bought passengers (some of them, at any rate) two nights in a brass bed rather than a berth; the opportunity to borrow books from a library in the observation car; sumptuous Fred Harvey meals in a spacious, 30-seat dining car paneled in vermillion mahogany; and the comfort produced by the first "air-cooling and air-washing device" ever installed in a rail car.

Ladies would receive an orchid corsage brought aboard near the California border by a flower boy, gentlemen an alligator wallet embossed in gold with the train's name. (These customs actually began in 1896 aboard Santa Fe's *California Limited,* another train with a pedigree.) Similar gracious amenities prevailed at times aboard the *AOE,* in the form of gifts such as lapel pins and backpacks, and returned with vigor on the *GrandLuxe Express* as shoulder bags and cobalt coffee cups. And larger than traditional bedrooms, showers, a library, and wood-paneled dining cars with exquisite food will all sound familiar to today's *GrandLuxe Express* passengers.

In the great days of train travel in North America, of course, a high degree of luxury was widespread, even the norm, when the Pullman Company reached every corner of the United States with its sleeping cars. More than one hundred thousand travelers a night were accommodated by the astonishing enterprise that George Mortimer Pullman founded. Great and evocative train names abounded, many of them attached to the famous "transcontinental" runs—a widely used misnomer, since until Amtrak extended its Los Angeles–New Orleans *Sunset Limited* to Florida on April 4, 1993 (an extension closed in August 2005 by Hurricane Katrina), no train actually spanned the North American continent. (Later came the *American Orient Express,* which ran public trips from Washington, D.C., to Sacramento in 1995. In 1996, and for a decade following, *AOE*'s "Great Transcontinental Journey" operated between Washington, D.C., and Los Angeles.)

But that quibble aside, the great so-called "transcontinental" trains were many. The *Overland Limited* traveled the route of the first transcontinental rail link, completed in 1869 by the driving of the golden spike at Promontory, Utah. Early in the streamliner era, preeminence on this Chicago & North Western–Union Pacific–Southern Pacific route (and other UP routes as well) was claimed by the fleet of "City" trains, which included the *City of Los Angeles* and *City of Portland,* whose dome cars would come to play peripheral roles in the *AOE* story.

To the north, Empire Builder James J. Hill's *Oriental Limited* on the Great Northern Railway is germane to this story, and not just for its name's similarity to "Orient Express." This luxurious St. Paul to Seattle service was inaugurated simultaneously with the launching of the Great Northern Steamship Company's *S.S. Minnesota* and *S.S. Dakota* in 1905, which realized Hill's longstanding ambition of linking his railroad with Asia. The *Oriental Limited* was extended east to Chicago in 1909, then replaced 20 years later as the premier train on the line by the *Empire Builder,* honoring Hill, one of the greatest railroaders in history. Worthy competitors in the Northwest were Northern Pacific's *North Coast Limited* and Chicago, Milwaukee, St. Paul & Pacific's *Olympian,* touted as a train "Fit for the Gods."

What could be expected aboard America's best trains in the golden age of rail travel? For many years a private room was a luxury, and open sections the vastly preponderant accommodation. In the rarest cases there might be a shower—public (though attended). There might be barber shops and train secretaries, designed to serve the harried businessman, and valets. There might be ladies' maids, hairdressers, manicurists.

Viewing the heritage question from a slightly different angle produces yet another nominee for the *GrandLuxe Express*'s true ancestor: the *California Zephyr.* Inaugurated in 1949, this Budd-built Chicago–San Francisco streamliner was touted as the first train to be scheduled for scenery. It was operated by three railroads in partnership: the Chicago, Burlington & Quincy, the Denver & Rio Grande Western, and the Western Pacific. Westbound, the train left Chicago in the afternoon, crossed the prairies overnight, then showed off the Rockies and successive canyons of the Colorado River throughout the next day. Scooting across the Nevada desert at night, the train arrived at dawn at the eastern approach to California's splendid Feather River Canyon.

With its five dome cars; delicious meals; attentive service, including Zephyrettes (hostesses who added an engaging human presence); comfortable and stylish equipment; and, perhaps best of all, the most scenic route of any train in America, the *CZ* was meant to be fun. And it surely was, living up to its self-applied moniker as "the most talked about train in the country."

What's in a name? "California Zephyr" says a lot. The name "Zephyr," which developed into a Burlington Route generic, came to company executives as they thumbed through the dictionary looking for "the last word" in passenger travel, and "California" spoke of destination. So did "Orient" in "Orient Express," even more powerfully.

Arguably the most famous train name in history, "Orient Express" has been much coveted and often copied. Though "GrandLuxe Express" in 2006 replaced "American Orient Express," which itself a dozen years earlier had replaced the original "American-European Express," the *Orient Express* remains a touchstone for the train's owners, and will continue to do so as long as the equipment that in 1989 launched the *AEE* is in service. With sleeping cars named "Istanbul" and "Paris," how could it not? And if diners *Chicago* and *Zurich,* with their dark wood paneling and delicate marquetry, don't remind you of a lost European elegance, they're simply not doing their job.

On October 4, 1883, the inaugural *Orient Express* (though at first officially called "Express d'Orient") left Paris's Gare de l'Est for Constantinople, today's Istanbul. Close to a century later, on May 27, 1977, the *Direct-Orient-Express* departed from Paris for Istanbul for the last time. By then it was a shoddy, pedestrian train, bereft of a dining car, and offering just a single sleeper and a few nondescript compartment cars. It was shorn of all that had made it famous save one thing: its name. But that was enough to generate a surprising amount of press attention around the world when the train died. And that attention was enough to set some people thinking.

What accounts for the fame and cachet that attached to this train throughout most of its nearly century-long career? For one thing, it surely got off on the right foot. From the beginning, it clearly wasn't meant for the common man. Rather, it was a train of the nobility, even royalty, a train of diplomats, aristocrats, millionaires, smugglers, and scoundrels. Its brilliant name was perfectly apt, since it brought the European traveler to the brink of the Bosporus, the gateway to Asia. And for endpoints, glamorous Paris and mysterious, exotic Constantinople couldn't be beat.

That the train has starred in literature and film obviously has helped build and promulgate its mystique, but this was probably as much the cart as the horse. Graham Greene's 1932 "entertainment," *Stamboul Train,* was set aboard, as was Agatha Christie's 1934 *Murder on the Orient Express,* which exactly four decades later became a film of the same name starring John Gielgud, with Albert Finney as detective Hercule Poirot. Alfred Hitchcock set his 1938 thriller *The Lady Vanishes* aboard the train, which also appeared more tangentially in many other books and movies, including Ian Fleming's *From Russia with Love.*

That first Constantinople-bound *Express d'Orient* was as diminutive as it was posh—exclusive in all ways. Powered by a tiny 2-4-0 belonging to Compagnie de l'Est, the train was just five cars long: two sleeping cars and a restaurant car, bracketed by *fourgons* (baggage cars). This little train was the pride of the grandly (yet appropriately) named "Compagnie Internationale des Wagons-Lits et des Grands Express Européens," the brainchild of Georges Nagelmackers, a Belgian engineer who would become Europe's George Pullman. The savvy Nagelmackers saw that this inaugural trip was made with hoopla and plenty of press coverage. In fact, one of the writers aboard, Edmond About, would write a whole book about the trip.

Nagelmackers was born in Liège in 1845. His was a family of bankers to King Leopold II, a connection that years later would prove invaluable to Nagelmackers as he undertook the complex and sensitive task of organizing cross-border sleeping-car service. The catalyst of his grand enterprise apparently was a visit to the United States in 1869, the year the first transcontinental railroad was completed. By that time Pullman had built his first sleeping car, the *Pioneer* (1865), and first dining car, the *Delmonico* (1868). Nagelmackers was impressed with the American's work, and he returned home determined to emulate Pullman's company, operating through sleeping cars not just on the lines of different railroads but through multiple countries.

In 1872 Nagelmackers formed the Compagnie Internationale des Wagons Lits ("et Grands Express Européens" was added a bit more than a decade later) and ordered the first sleeping cars built in Europe, primitive vehicles riding on four wheels, typical of European railway cars at the time. (In America, passenger coaches already used four-wheel trucks, an innovation held suspect in Europe until 1883.) In 1873 Nagelmackers joined forces with the flamboyant American entrepreneur Colonel William d'Alton Mann to form Mann's Railway Sleeping Car Company. When Nagelmackers bought Mann's interest in the company three years later, he became sole owner of 53 seductively named "Mann Boudoir Sleeping Cars."

At a conference held in early 1883 in Constantinople, Nagelmackers and representatives of the eight railway companies that initially would handle the train between Paris and Constantinople agreed that the train would consist of two or more sleeping cars (the "Wagons-Lits," or "bed cars," of the company name), a restaurant car, and two baggage cars, one of which would be used for mail. When the first—unofficial, uninaugurated—*Express d'Orient* ran in June, only from Paris to Vienna, the cars were small, six-wheel vehicles. But when the train left Gare de l'Est for the first time officially, the two *wagons-lits* and the *wagon-restaurant* were larger cars that rolled on trucks.

Opulent they were, too. The restaurant car, which had separate small lounges for men and women in addition to the dining tables for four or two (and thus officially considered a "*wagon-salon-restaurant*"), was paneled in wood dense with ornamentation. The restaurant chairs were of dark embossed leather, accented with brass studs. Carpeting was dark red. Broad windows were hung with curtains of pleated damask.

Lighting was by gas lamp. Food was exquisite, and service featured fine china, silver, and crystal. And the two sleeping cars, with 42 beds, were commensurately swank.

A list of the railroads involved in handling the train on its three-day-plus journey makes clear the complexity of Nagelmackers's undertaking, and puts in perspective the nonetheless daunting task GrandLuxe Rail Journeys faces today in dealing with a handful of freight railroads. After the train left Paris on the rails of Compagnie de l'Est, ahead still lay the Imperial Management of the Alsace-Lorraine Railways, the State Railways of the Grand Duchy of Baden, the State Railway of the Kingdom of Württemberg, the Lines of Communication of the Kingdom of Bavaria, the State Railways of Vienna, the Imperial and Royal Austrian State Railways, and the Royal General Management of Rumanian Railways. (Though all these lines were developed independently, they did connect, and all were built in standard gauge and ran compatible equipment, apparently for strategic military reasons. On the other hand, it's said that the tsars dictated broad gauge for Russia as protection against invasion.)

And that litany of lines took the early *Orient Express* traveler only to Giurgi on the Rumanian bank of the Danube, where the journey would take a turn for the worse. Passengers would board a ferry to cross the river to Rustchuk in Bulgaria, where they boarded far less luxurious coaches to journey to Varna, on the Black Sea. There the steamer *Espero* waited to embark now less-pampered patrons on a sometimes tumultuous 18-hour voyage to Constantinople. In 1889 the rail line was completed all the way to Constantinople, and the *Orient Express* became all luxury, all the way.

Many changes lay ahead for this famous train, in both equipment and route, but nothing could dull its glamour—short of the public's changing transportation preferences, which is what finally occurred. But before that, coaches would continue to get bigger and better. They'd be made of steel and lighted by electricity. They would have vestibules, which made movement between the cars safer and more comfortable. Improvements would continue in an unbroken upward arc right through the 1920s, when cars were built that, in some cases, survived into the 1970s. This evolution culminated with 90 steel carriages in the LX, or Luxe, series, built in 1929, some in England and some in France. These cars, which had the largest sleeping compartments ever operated in Europe, were wood-paneled throughout and featured exquisite marquetry, often Art Deco in style, by René Prou and other designers.

It is these cars that provided the model for the cars of the *American-European Express.*

Unlike the evolution of rolling stock, shifts in route and operations were more tangled than linear, triggered in part by two world wars (the *Orient Express* was suspended during both) and the realignment of borders, even nations, that resulted from each. In particular, the Treaty of Versailles dictated the rerouting of the *Orient Express* to avoid Germany and Austria. Thus was born, on April 11, 1919, the *Simplon-Orient-Express,* using the newly opened Simplon Tunnel between Switzerland and Italy.

The next pertinent chapter in the *Orient Express* story was written by a pair of Swiss cousins, Edy Zuger and Alby Glatt, who later would be central players in the saga of the European train's American cousin. This chapter opened in 1977, the year of the demise of the original *Orient Express.* Both Zuger and Glatt were then with the major Swiss transportation company Intraflug AG, of which Glatt was president and chairman. Glatt would also become owner and operator of a new Zurich-based tour train, the *Nostalgie Istanbul Orient Express,* with Zuger as chief executive officer.

Some five years earlier, Glatt and Zuger had begun to acquire a rake of the classic Wagons-Lits sleepers and restore them. Typically, beginning in 1977, the *NIOE* would make two regularly scheduled excursions annually from Paris to Istanbul in emulation of its historic forebear. In addition, the train was available for charter. In 1988, it undertook what was touted as the longest continuous rail trip on record—from Paris to Hong Kong via Germany, Poland, Russia, and China. From Hong Kong the train was transshipped to Tokyo.

In time, another reincarnation of the *Orient Express* would come to overshadow the *NIOE*—the *Venice Simplon-Orient-Express,* created by James B. Sherwood, head of the Sea Containers Group. An auction in October 1977 in Monaco of five elegant Wagons-Lits carriages from the twenties by Sotheby Parke Bernet caught Sherwood's interest, already piqued by the publicity surrounding the last run of the *Orient Express* the previous May. He attended the auction and managed to buy two of these cars, then began a search throughout Europe that eventually netted another 16, most of them the exquisite Luxe series sleepers.

Not content with that, he acquired eight British Pullmans, equally plush and filled with wood and marquetry, so that his passengers could begin in London, a prime tourist destination, travel to Folkestone on the English Channel, cross by ship to Boulogne, and then join the

Wagons-Lits rake to travel to Paris and then on overnight to Venice. (Alternate itineraries would evolve as well, including occasional trips all the way to Istanbul.) Both trains, which began operation in 1982 and are still going strong today, are rolling museums.

Eventually, Sherwood's *VSOE* and what was then Henry Hillman's *AOE* would butt heads over rights to the name "Orient Express," and Sherwood would win.

photo gallery

In June of 1936, the heavyweight *20th Century Limited* rolls north at Hudson, New York, in a view taken from the rear of the New York City–bound *Cayuga*. The open-platform observation was a staple of the great trains of the era. *The Edward L. May Memorial Collection, courtesy Richard Stoving.*

The *Overland Limited*, touted as the only extra-fare train between Chicago and San Francisco, had a woody ambiance that could have been a prototype for the *AOE*. The diner, with its four and two seating, and the buffet-library, were the cuspidors removed, could put you in mind of *Zurich, Chicago, Rocky Mountain,* and *Seattle.* No barber wanted on the *AOE,* but there are many more showers than the *Overland* claimed. *Karl Zimmermann Collection.*

Southwest Indian art and design enhance the Budd-built cars of the 1937 *Super Chief*: lounge *Acoma,* where the steward pours a glass of beer, and observation-lounge *Navajo. Santa Fe Railway.*

Santa Fe was very clear to whom it was marketing in its advertising for the *de Luxe*—to the very wealthy, and perhaps those who wished they were. *Santa Fe Railway.*

BELOW: The Union Pacific and Chicago & North Western's *City of Denver*, seen here in Denver in April 1942, was among the earliest full-sized streamliners. *Union Pacific Railroad.*

ABOVE: The *California Zephyr* is nearing the end of its career as it snakes eastbound through Colorado's Gore Canyon in the summer of 1969. *Laurel Zimmermann.*

FACING PAGE: The Budd Company, builder of Burlington's substantial *Zephyr* fleet, was proud of the *California Zephyr,* generally regarded as the greatest of the lot. *Karl Zimmermann Collection.*

A great new train — **THE CALIFORNIA ZEPHYR**

Three railroads—the Burlington, the Denver & Rio Grande Western, and the Western Pacific—are placing in operation on March 20th six all-stainless steel trains built by Budd, to provide a new daily service between Chicago and San Francisco over a scenic route of incomparable grandeur.

These are the spectacular new California Zephyrs—trains of almost unbelievable beauty and luxury. Their Vista-Domes, de-luxe coaches, cars reserved for women and children, lounges, diners and most modern of all transcontinental sleepers offer travel enjoyment beyond your dreams.

The California Zephyrs traverse some of the finest scenery in the world, and their schedules, in both directions, permit you to enjoy the most exciting portions during daylight hours ... the serried peaks of the highest Colorado Rockies ... Gore and Glenwood Canyons ... snowy Sierras ... and California's fabulous Feather River Canyon of gold rush fame.

Another incentive to travel on these wonderful trains is the fact that they are constructed, not merely sheathed, with stainless steel, the strongest material used in building railway cars. Beneath their gleaming surface these cars have structures of the same lustrous metal, three times as strong as ordinary steel. In the United States, the only all-stainless steel cars are built by Budd ... and Budd builds no other kind. The Budd Company, Philadelphia 32, Pa.

The *Venice Simplon-Orient-Express* curves east through the Austrian Alps, then pauses at Anton am Arlberg. *Karl Zimmermann.*

This *VSOE* diner, built in 1929 as a first-class Pullman, was designed by René Lalique in the "Côte d'Azur" style. The "Bacchanalian maidens" glass panel was the highlight.
Karl Zimmermann.

The raised Wagons-Lits crest adorned the finest sleepers of Europe. *Karl Zimmermann.*

It's teatime aboard the *Bournemouth Belle,* a day excursion operated by *VSOE* when its Pullman rake was not busy ferrying through passengers to Folkestone. Gold-striped cream and brown was the traditional livery of British Pullman service. *Karl Zimmermann.*

FACING PAGE: Neither the *American-European Express* nor the *American Orient Express* often saw a snowy setting like this one at Chicago Union Station on December 30, 1990. The train has been wyed after its arrival and is backing into the station. This is one of its few trips with streamlined diesels, led by F-units that once belonged to the Clinchfield Railroad. *Bruce C. Nelson.*

2

The *American-European Express* Comes and Goes

N o train compares with this show train," sang John Wallowitch, seated at a shiny black Baldwin baby grand piano aboard lounge car *Bay Point Club,* hurtling north from Washington on the tail end of Amtrak No. 188, the *Embassy.* Dressed in black tie, with a white silk scarf slung smartly around his neck, Wallowitch perfectly exemplified the savvy elegance that *Bay Point Club's* owners had in mind. Finishing his Noel Cowardesque paean to his train—the *American-European Express*—Wallowitch smiled coyly. "I wrote it this afternoon on the plane from Chicago," he said.

The date was November 9, 1989, and *Bay Point Club,* along with diner *Chicago* and sleeper *Istanbul,* would the following week begin a regular Washington-Chicago schedule. That day, however, they were headed for New York City's Pennsylvania Station for a few days of preening for the press and travel-industry professionals. In the lounge, with the wheels-on-rail sounds of high-speed railroading on the Northeast Corridor a muted undercurrent to Wallowitch's sophisticated cocktail piano, champagne was passed in tall crystal flutes, along with hot hors d'oeuvres. Softly lit and elegant in every way, *Bay Point Club* was clearly intended to recall the luxury of the *Orient Express.* Travelers on this pre-inaugural special could never have guessed this club car's humble origins—as a Union Pacific 14-section sleeper, already outmoded by the time it was delivered in 1954.

What they saw instead of the one-time pastel walls and berth curtains was a vision of plush Art Deco splendor that builder American Car & Foundry could never have predicted 35 years earlier. At one end of the spacious lounge that ran most of the car's length was an ebony bar with black granite top; on the bar front was the intertwined *AEE* crest. In mid-car stood the Baldwin baby grand, on which was perched a splashy bouquet of fresh flowers. The embossed fabric of the side walls was "Jockey Leather," supplied by Brunschwig & Fils of North White Plains, New York, a century-old French fabric house. This firm, which provided fabrics for all the *AEE* cars, claims among its projects the presidential yacht *Sequoia.*

The car's ceiling—deep indigo and purple, showing clouds on the horizon aglow with dying daylight—was strewn with 23-karat-gold stars. Fans whirred quietly overhead. The guests took all this in from comfortable sofas and club chairs, before moving into diner *Chicago,* where tables were laid with fine Belgian damask tablecloths and napkins and china bearing the company logo. Crystal by Mikasa and oversized European flatware by Oneida completed the elegant settings.

Chicago had a luxuriantly ornate main section with four-and-two seating for 26 and a separate executive dining room (which could be rented for meetings) at the end of the car with two tables for five. *Chicago* and sister diner *Zurich*—similar, but seating 40 rather than 36— were paneled in Honduran mahogany with delicate marquetry; ceilings were faux marble; and windows were hung with richly textured balloon shades. In the main dining area, silver table lamps with silk shades glowed cozily. Edgar F. Zappel, *chef de train,* came through the dining car, stopping at tables to chat about the amenities the *AEE* would offer when it entered service the following week.

"Your porter is your personal butler," he said, "available to polish shoes or sew on a missing button. The chefs? They come from the Culinary Institute of America."

This sprint from Washington to Manhattan was, in effect, the *American-European Express*'s coming-out party. It was a bold, auspicious debut, but the road ahead for this stylish train would be rough and convoluted indeed.

⁂

The decade of the nineties in the United States was littered with the corpses of failed luxury trains—upscale operations functioning outside of (or collateral with) the workaday world of Amtrak. The *California Sun Express,* a Princess Cruises–operated ex–Milwaukee Road full-length dome that tagged along behind Amtrak's *Coast Starlight* on its Los Angeles-San Francisco leg: RIP, 1990. Transcisco Tours' garishly painted San Jose-Reno *Sierra 49er Express:* RIP, 1991; Amtrak's own New York City-Pittsburgh *Keystone Classic Club,* an adjunct of its *Pennsylvanian:* RIP, 1992. The less fancy *Florida Fun Train:* RIP, 1998. And it didn't end in the nineties. The *Acadian:* RIP, 2003. *Montana Daylight:* RIP, 2005. Nor start there. *20th Century Rail Tours:* RIP, 1982.

The most substantial, most visible, and thus generally most lamented failure came in October 1991, however, when this *American-European Express* that had begun with such high hopes threw in the towel after roughly two years of operation—years bedeviled at first by uncertainty on market and mission, inconsistent (and sometimes downright paltry) ridership, and an expensive derailment. But the cars rebuilt for the *AEE* have had staying power. They became the *American Orient Express* and remain the core of GrandLuxe Rail's train.

The *American-European Express* did get off to a brave start on November 15, offering six-nights-a-week service between Washington and Chicago. *AEE*'s luxurious cars—the lounge, the diner, and (when running at full capacity) three sleepers—operated as part of Amtrak's *Capitol Limited.* (Choice of Washington and Chicago as endpoints apparently had as much to do with finding an Amtrak train that could handle five additional cars as with any carefully honed marketing plan.) *AEE* was clearly selling transportation, though of the most elegant sort, and business travelers were targeted at least as prominently as vacationers.

The project had its roots back in 1977, when Alby Glatt inaugurated the *Nostalgie Istanbul Orient Express,* that Zurich-based tour train made up of historic carriages, most once belonging to Wagons-Lits. In 1986, Glatt and Edy Zuger, chief executive officer of *NIOE,* approached William F. Spann, managing partner of the Bay Point Yacht and Country Club in Panama City, Florida, about developing a luxury train in the United States. Spann was receptive, because he'd had a soft spot for overnight trains ever since his boyhood, when he often rode from South Carolina to Florida with his family aboard the Atlantic Coast Line's *East Coast Champion.*

"The Champion left Florence at 2 AM," he reminisced, "but even as a child who seldom stayed up past *I Love Lucy,* I always climbed up to the vestibule wide awake. I knew there would be excitement waiting. There would be porters, pillows. Ice cold water, mysterious strangers, and endless railroad stories. There would be blue night lights, long shadows, a sleepy sunrise, and towns which passed by huge windows in pace with the timetable."

So the plan went forward.

"The members' lounge at Bay Point Yacht and Country Club seems a remote location for the birth of America's only regularly scheduled luxury train," Spann recalled in 1989, when the *AEE* began service. "But it was there three years ago that the owners of the *Nostalgie Istanbul Orient Express* and I agreed to pursue the development of the *American-European Express.* What started with a quiet handshake, an exchange of commitments to excellence, and a toast of fine champagne grew to an international effort of extraordinary proportions."

Investors had to be found, which turned out to be no simple task.

"The first step was to convince European and American money markets," Spann said, "that the concept of an American train deluxe was, in fact, a survivable business equation. The first bankers to hear the idea responded with cautious chuckles and outright denials." Eventually sufficient investors were found, and the search was begun that eventually located 13 1940s and 1950s railroad cars appropriate for rebuilding. Ten of these were actually refurbished, with mechanical work on six done at Northern Rail Car Company near Milwaukee and four at Kasten Railcar Services outside St. Louis. The stylish décor was provided by Bay Point Interiors of Panama City, and in particular Melissa Spann—wife of Bill Spann, who had assumed the presidency of *AEE,* while Glatt had become chairman of the board.

These ten cars, plus a very important one to come, refurbished for *AEE* service at a cost of $1 million or more apiece (the 11 had a value of $14 million all told), represented as posh a train as this country had ever seen. The *AEE* was indeed remarkable, though not particularly for the opulence of its sleeping quarters, which—in spite of wood paneling, faux marble in the toilet annexes, and framed art—offered mostly the double bedrooms that had been the standard rail accommodation for two for half a century or more. Instead, *AEE's* most notable feature was the elegance of its diners and lounges, all turned into silk purses from the sows' ears of workaday late-1940s and 1950s streamliners. Though the sleepers were somewhat reconfigured in 1996, some club and dining car furniture rearranged, and the upholstery throughout renewed frequently, the train produced in 1989 by Kasten Railcar and Northern Rail Car—and, most significantly in terms of aesthetics, by Bay Point Interiors, Tom Ethridge (whose Ethridge Cabinet Shop was responsible for the fine wood paneling and marquetry), and Melissa Spann—is basically the *American Orient Express* that greeted the millennium, before operations were expanded to include an *AOE II.*

Since the *American-European Express* was initially two trains, it comprised five pairs of cars: sleepers *Monte Carlo* and *Washington* (8 bedrooms and crew quarters), *Paris* and *Istanbul* (7 bedrooms, 2 drawing rooms, and an office for the *chef de train*), and *Vienna* and *Berlin* (9 bedrooms, 1 presidential cabin); club cars *St. Moritz* and *Bay Point*

Club; and diners *Chicago* and *Zurich.* The two diners were similar in décor, as were the club cars—though *St. Moritz,* appropriately for the namesake of a resort in the Swiss Alps, had a mural of snowcapped mountains lining the curve to its ceiling. (Details of the histories of these cars, and their modifications through the years, can be found in chapter 5.)

Staffing was both generous in number and high in quality. Zappel came to AEE with seven years of experience at the Bay Point Yacht and Country Club. Serving no more than 56 travelers was the staff of a dozen reporting to him: *chef de cuisine,* sous-chef, utility person, chief steward, two dining-car waiters, a server and a bartender in the club car, a piano player, and three porters, one for each sleeping car.

"To the first call for on-board staff in Chicago," Spann recalled, "came the response of over five hundred eager, potential train employees."

One individual who would become deeply involved with the *American Orient Express* in later years entered the *AEE* picture right at the beginning: John Kirkwood, founder in 1983 of Rail Ventures, a company that offers private rail cars for charter and lease. As excitement built for the November 15 start-up, it became clear that work in Panama City on the interiors of sleepers *Monte Carlo* and *Vienna* would not be completed on time. Bill Spann then located Kirkwood and arranged to lease two of his cars as stand-ins: *Yerba Buena* and *Bella Vista,* the latter of which would have a long history with *AEE* and later *AOE.*

Yerba Buena was built in 1942 by Pullman-Standard as sleeper *Imperial Drive* for Overland Route service; it was later rebuilt by Autoliner to business-car configuration, with open platform, lounge, dining room, and bedrooms. A memorable moment for the car came on an early *AEE* trip when its dining room served as a moving studio for the taping of an episode of the *Oprah Winfrey Show.* Though Spann and others were disappointed that the train and journey were little more than background for Oprah's chat, it must have provided some useful exposure for the new enterprise (though, in fact, the train was broadly and positively reported in news and feature stories in newspapers and magazines generally). And the occasion proved a propitious one for Art Smith, *AEE*'s first executive chef. Oprah liked his cooking so much that she hired him as her personal chef. Smith has gone on to become a celebrity chef, cookbook author, and television personality.

The splendid color scheme still worn by GrandLuxe cars—goldstriped cream and blue, a streamliner-era classic—was introduced by *American-European Express.* The *AEE* logo easily and gracefully would morph into *AOE.* The handsome gold-rimmed, blue-banded china—designed by Richard Luckin, dining-car-china guru and video producer—on *AEE* easily worked for *AOE* with just a tweak of one logo letter and now serves for GrandLuxe Rail with a "GLR." (Service in the dining cars became even more stylish later when *AOE* introduced eye-catching chargers in 1996.)

The *American-European Express* was very clearly positioned as the stateside running mate of the *Nostalgie Istanbul Orient Express*. The *AEE* logo, brochure lettering, and tag line "Railway Train Deluxe" all replicated the *NIOE*'s. Literature often carried the notation "Operated in cooperation with the Nostalgie Istanbul Orient Express." *AEE* brochures advertised the *NIOE*, "the mother of modern deluxe rail service," as "the sister train of the *American-European Express*."

In contradistinction to the decidedly casual atmosphere that eventually evolved aboard the *American Orient Express,* the *AEE* was a consciously dressy train. This was spelled out in its passenger guide: "In both Club and Dining Cars, jackets and ties are required of gentlemen during evening travel. Black tie is popular among gentlemen for evening service." No doubt a similar dressiness was encouraged aboard the *NIOE*. Certainly it was and still is aboard the *Venice Simplon-Orient-Express*.

In spite of rarefied service, however, ridership never developed for *AEE* on this initial route. (Though the company explained that the cost of travel between Washington and Chicago in a bedroom—$695 for one person, $1,042.50 for two—compared favorably with the aggregate cost of a first-class air ticket, overnight stay in a luxury hotel, and gourmet dinner, it still seemed high to most. An Amtrak bedroom for two on the *Capitol Limited* cost $434.) In May 1990, Washington-Chicago service was dropped to tri-weekly, and twice-weekly service between New York and Chicago in the consist of the *Broadway Limited* was added. This change was small improvement, however. Business travelers, apparently, were just not interested in spending an unnecessary night on the road, whether in high style or not. Probably the idea of taking an overnight train on business was just too outlandish to get serious consideration.

And somehow these two routes were insufficiently interesting to tourists, though New York, Chicago, and Washington are arguably America's three greatest cities, and Philadelphia surely is replete with history and interest. In collaboration with seven hotels in those four cities, the train began to offer packages, such as "The Vacation Plan," which included three hotel nights at the destination city. Still aiming at the business traveler, "The Chief Executive Officer" combined a single room on the train with a return flight on American Airlines, and a similar combination was offered for couples traveling. "The Romantic Interlude" added private limousine service and a two-night hotel stay. "The Family Plan" offered a discount for two adults traveling with one or two children 6 to 16 years old.

As a sideline, *AEE* offered charter travel in conjunction with Kirkwood's Rail Ventures. "Private Car Exclusive Service," the charter option was called, "for two to twenty." The feature car was the open-platform observation *Yerba Buena,* which had been used at the *AEE* start-up while the last of its own cars were completed. For larger groups, sleeper *Bella Vista* (another early stand-in for *AEE*'s own cars) could be included. Staffing was with *AEE* personnel, and Kirkwood's cars were described as "designed to reflect the elegance of the *American-European Express.*"

In fact, all Rail Ventures cars that *AEE* leased—in addition to *Yerba Buena* and *Bella Vista,* these would include sleeper *Montecito* and sleeper-buffet lounge *Monterey*—had been refurbished in Panama City and were equipped similarly—same linens and details and amenities—to the *AEE* cars.

"I intentionally made them compatible," Kirkwood recalled later, a decision that would prove a lucky one for *AEE* and later *AOE.* In fact, Spann and Kirkwood at one time had serious discussions about operating *Yerba Buena, Bella Vista,* and *Montecito* as an adjunct to the *AEE,* connecting with it at Chicago and serving Los Angeles via Amtrak's *Southwest Chief.* They eventually abandoned the idea, concluding that "you couldn't mix products successfully," in Kirkwood's words.

So the main thrust of course remained the Washington-Chicago and New York-Chicago service, until both were suspended in November 1990 because of inadequate bookings. But on March 1, 1991, the *American-European Express* would be up and running again, this time with a whole new concept: a 24-hour "land cruise" between New York and Chicago via the scenic CSX (former Chesapeake & Ohio) route through the New River Gorge. The luxurious Greenbrier, the C&O resort at White Sulphur Springs, West Virginia, was the destination that would make the newly constituted service work for tourists. In addition, *AEE* astutely shifted its marketing focus from the independent traveler to groups and those who could be lured by packages with airlines and hotels.

The *Greenbrier Limited,* as the newly deployed train would be called, had been kicked off with much hoopla on December 21, 1990, when a combined consist—five sleepers, a lounge, and two diners (though just one, *Chicago,* appropriately, was in service)—left Chicago Union Station's Track 20, bound for White Sulphur Springs and Washington, with Bill Spann aboard as host. The joint aegis of the train's new incarnation was made clear by the card of greeting found aboard, which read, in part, "American-European Express and CSX Transportation welcome all passengers and invited guests aboard the Inaugural Expedition of the Greenbrier Limited." Further evidence of the partnership with CSX was the special's motive power: CSX's ex-Clinchfield F7's, A-unit No. 116 and B-unit No. 117, joined by a MARC F-unit, needed to provide head-end power, which the two former freight units could not. Another sign of CSX's enthusiasm for this partnership was its assignment of numbers 1 and 2 to the *Greenbrier Limited,* a clear statement to the operating department that the train was to be given priority.

Among the "invited guests" was journalist Bob Johnston, who covered the inaugural for *Passenger Train Journal.* From Spann, he learned that Ted Kleisner, president and managing director of The Greenbrier, had been the catalyst in forming the partnership between train and resort.

"Ted picked up the phone one day," Spann told Johnston, "and asked, 'Why are you running up there?'" By "up there" he of course meant the more northerly ex–Baltimore & Ohio route of the *Capitol* and ex–Pennsylvania Railroad route of the *Broadway.*

In any case, The Greenbrier and the *AEE* were a good match, elegance meeting elegance. In 1910 the Chesapeake & Ohio Railway had bought the Grand Central Hotel and the cottage community that surrounded it at White Sulphur Springs, all of which developed because of the reputed healing powers of the hot springs there. That same year C&O began building the central portion of what is today's hotel, a National Historic Landmark, to attract tourists and build its passenger revenues—a story reminiscent of the construction of national park lodges by such railroads as the Santa Fe (working together with Fred Harvey), Great Northern, Northern Pacific, and Union Pacific. A particularly apt analogy is the grand Banff Springs Hotel, opened at its Alberta location (like White Sulphur, a hot springs) in 1888 by the Canadian Pacific Railway to generate tourist traffic.

Like the Banff Springs, The Greenbrier is among North America's premier resorts. Robert R. Young, whose impetuosity would also figure tangentially in the equipment side of the *AEE* story, recounted later, was C&O chairman in the post–World War II years. He oversaw an upgrading of the hotel (which had been sold by C&O to the U.S. Army during the war for use as a hospital and then repurchased) that cost millions of dollars. Time has shown this to have been a far better investment than the overabundance of passenger cars he ordered during the same period.

For the twice-weekly *Greenbrier Limited,* the combined *AEE* consists for the first time would be run as an independent train, under CSX auspices except between New York and Washington. There, for the trains traversing the Northeast Corridor on weekdays (a Tuesday departure from Chicago and Thursday from New York), only some cars (two sleepers, a diner, and the observation car) would be handled as part of Amtrak's *Congressional* (Nos. 183 and 186). For the Friday Chicago and Sunday New York departures, which made their Corridor passages on the weekend, the entire consist would run through as a stand-alone train. (The practice of not running the complete train on the Corridor on weekdays stemmed from *AEE*'s gentlemen's agreement not to compete with Amtrak's Metroliners.)

Though the Metroliners and *AEE* might seem deeply disparate carriers, *AEE* did indeed offer parlor-car as well as sleeping-car service. In fact, day service between New York or Washington and The Greenbrier was an important aspect in the train's loadings. Many passengers carried to White Sulphur Springs in this way would, after their hotel stays, either continue on overnight to Chicago on *AEE* or return in parlor accommodations to Washington or New York. Parlor passengers were carried aboard the *New York* observation (once it entered service on May 3), the mid-train club cars, or sometimes in sleeping rooms sold as day space. Other travelers simply made the through journey to Chicago. This variety of options was helpful in filling the train, which typically ran at 90 percent of capacity, though it could make inventory management complex.

After the festive *Greenbrier Limited* inaugural, the train made a round trip to Chicago to celebrate New Year's Eve, then headed for Panama City to thaw out. To get the train in position for a Valentine's Day special to The Greenbrier, management offered an intriguing one-time-only excursion from Panama City to Chicago on February 9 and 10. Billed as "The Heart of the South Limited," with clarinetist Buddy DeFranco performing on board, the train left on its hometown Bay Line Railroad—an interesting short line, formerly the Atlanta & St. Andres Bay Railway, which once hosted through sleeping-car service from Panama City to Atlanta. From Dothan, Alabama, CSX forwarded the "Limited" to Chicago. (The day before departure for Chicago, the train had run to Dothan and back as a fund-raiser for United Way.)

The *Greenbrier Limited* was given stylish bookends, though never at the same time. On the head end, though only briefly, were those ex-Clinchfield F's. Carrying the markers, eventually, was the *New York,* a beautifully refurbished observation car with heritage and cachet. It had begun life in 1948 as the *20th Century Limited*'s *Sandy Creek,* built by Pullman-Standard. A head-end car, to be called "London," was projected but never completed. This ex–Union Pacific boiler-dormitory car was to be rebuilt with a health club (including exercise room, sauna, and masseuse) and would also serve as a baggage car and generate head-end power. Renovations were begun at Northern Rail Car but stopped when *AEE* was forced to suspend operations.

Though "London" was stillborn, the car named for that British city's transatlantic rival, New York, was born and thrived, but only after a long and complex pregnancy.

"Put it in a museum or scrap it." That had been the disheartening initial assessment of *Sandy Creek* by Eric B. Levin, *AEE*'s general mechanical superintendent, when he inspected the car in early 1990 at the Northern Rail Car facilities in Cudahy, Wisconsin. "It appeared to me to be unfit for restoration or re-manufacture," Levin said.

After being briefly in the hands of Ringling Bros. and Barnum & Bailey, the car had passed through various owners, during which time it fell prey to the elements and vandals. After an exterior restoration, it was given in 1976 to the Indiana Transportation Museum, which a dozen years later sold it to Kasten Railcar. *AEE* got the car from Kasten as part of a business settlement. After examining it, Levin was definitely not sanguine about its future—a viewpoint he dutifully passed on to Bill Spann.

"I got a letter back," Levin recalled, "and it said 'fix the car.' So fix it we did." Work was done at Northern Rail Car, but all the engineering was directly supervised by *AEE*—not the case with the work on the initial ten cars done at Northern and Kasten. Along the way to being transformed to *New York, Sandy Creek* was stripped entirely. The sides were sawn off six inches below the window band and reframed. Two kinks were taken out of the center sill of the car, which received new trucks from a former Grand Trunk Western diner. There were some carbody modifications. A commissary door midway on the car's side was blanked and replaced by a small package-loading door. Since the car's five double bedrooms would be removed and replaced by swivel parlor seats for revenue service, windows were added to the former aisle side at the car's bedroom end.

New York was little but a shell when it was sent to Panama City,

A TALE OF TWO CREEKS

On September 15, 1948, one of the country's greatest trains—New York Central's *20th Century Limited*—appeared newly imagined, ready to begin one last push for the American passenger trade, on the New York-Chicago run in particular. The train's feature cars were its observations *Hickory Creek* and *Sandy Creek,* Pullman-Standard products like the rest of the train.

The *Creek* cars ran for just 19 years in *Century* service, and now more than twice that number have passed since the *20th Century Limited* died on December 2, 1967, shorn of its famous name and stylish observation cars. The *Creek* cars' time on the *Century* was largely uneventful, the only notable change coming in 1961 when the interiors of their lounges were refurbished and reconfigured as part of an upgrade of services made to help celebrate the train's sixtieth birthday the following year. Since their retirement from the *Century,* however, both cars have led adventurous lives, full of ups and downs—the ups coming most recently.

Sandy Creek, of course, eventually became the *New York,* and (if you don't discount the few years of inactivity while *AEE* was passing the baton to *AOE*), *New York* will soon have more service time for *AEE* and successors than *Sandy Creek* had for the Central. And since 2002, when *Hickory Creek*'s cosmetic restoration was essentially completed to its 1948 as-built appearance (and especially since 2005, when mechanical work allowed the car to begin running), devotees of these distinguished cars have had the opportunity to compare NYC's original, cleanlined interior with *AEE*'s lush makeover.

While *Sandy Creek* passed only briefly through Ringling Bros. ownership, *Hickory Creek* ran for years in the consist of one of the circus trains. Eventually the car went out of service and into storage at the circus's rail facility in Venice, Florida, where both wet weather and vandalism took a heavy toll. Windows were smashed. The door and diaphragm disappeared, along with water tank and essential pieces of the air-conditioning system. The interior was scrawled with graffiti. Due largely to window leakage, body rot set in.

An equipment broker acquired the car in 1990, then sought advice from Walter Grosselfinger, founder (in 1986) of the United Railroad Historical Society of New Jersey. Did he know of a historical group in the Northeast that might have the interest and wherewithal to preserve this significant car? Grosselfinger told Ray Clauss, who had a decade of experience rebuilding railroad equipment, of the car, and the connections were made that would eventually bring *Hickory Creek* back to life for URHS.

In 1991 the battered hulk that was *Hickory Creek* moved north, where Clauss began preliminary restoration, which continued sporadically until the big break came: New Jersey's approval of URHS's 1997 application for a grant under the Intermodal Surface Transportation Enhancement Act (ISTEA). Of the $650,000 expended to restore the car, $617,000 came from that grant.

The work required was monumental: repair and replacement of the crash posts at the vestibule end; replacement of the steps, which were beyond repair; of the side sills; and of the curved side sheets at the observation end—all this and much more. Finally, the car was primed and the skin filled and re-sanded three times to ensure a smooth finish. And then there was extensive interior work—filling what was virtually an empty shell—to make the car look like new.

"Seeing the car emerge once again in its original livery was unbelievable," Grosselfinger said. "At first it wore a solid, Pennsy-Tuscan–like primer. Then came the masking for the stripes, and the black-outlined silver for the lettering, then the grays, the lighter one first, then the darker." But the pièce de résistance came more than a year later.

"When that classic, blue-lighted tailsign was finally hung on the rear," Grosselfinger added, "it gave me chills."

Observation *New York* at the South Rim of Grand Canyon. *Karl Zimmermann.*

BELOW LEFT: The "Lookout Lounge" aboard restored *Hickory Creek,* showing its rather stark as-built appearance. *Karl Zimmermann.*

BELOW RIGHT: The "Lookout Lounge" aboard *AEE*'s *New York. Karl Zimmermann.*

Hickory Creek speeds south toward New York City on what had been the route of the *20th Century Limited* in August 2005. *Karl Zimmermann, both photos.*

where interior work by Tom Ethridge and Melissa Spann would complete the $1.5 million restoration. "The only thing left intact was the curved ceiling in the observation end," according to Levin. If it was a blank slate, Ethridge and Spann filled it beautifully. Above a wooden wainscot was a blue-green patterned wall covering; above that was a wooden indirect-lighting valence, with sweeping horizontal accents the color of burnished aluminum. The result was a total transformation of a tattered hulk (albeit a famous one) into a surpassingly opulent car.

This same small miracle had, in fact, been accomplished for each of *New York*'s ten running mates.

The one common thread running through the entire history of the luxury train is Gregory E. Mueller. He was aboard the inaugural trip in 1989 and is the single person who has been involved in every phase of the train's evolution and has worked with all of the principals.

Since Mueller was a proponent of the "land cruise" concept from the very beginning, it's appropriate that his connection with *AEE* was forged aboard the historic steamboat *Delta Queen*. Mueller had worked for the Delta Queen Steamboat Company in various capacities for a number of years, initially as chief purser and later handling special projects. (Mueller's first transportation love was actually aviation, since Southwest Air Rangers was his family's business.)

"Edy Zuger was enamored of both steamboats and the American West," according to Mueller, and a steamboat colleague of Mueller's introduced the two. Zuger and Mueller found themselves simpatico, and Mueller eventually expanded what was first a consultant role with *AEE* to full-time work with the company as an officer and director.

Intertwined with an ongoing career with Currey Adkins Cook, a Texas consulting firm, Mueller later would be president of *American Orient Express* for three of its formative years and, later still, vice-chairman of GrandLuxe Rail Journeys.

The confluence of interests and personalities is intriguing. During the mid-1980s, multiple entities in the travel and tourism industries felt that North America needed and could support a luxury overnight passenger train. Thomas Rader was working with Princess Cruise Lines while developing a project called "Golden Eagle" on his own, Spann and the Swiss cousins were planning the *American-European Express,* and Mueller with Delta Queen Steamboat Company was developing the "Grand American Railway" project. While Spann envisioned regularly scheduled service on select routes behind Amtrak trains, something like what the Pullman Company offered in its finest years, Rader and Mueller were more focused on multiple-night land cruises that ranged across North America.

It was in late 1982 that some senior officers from the *Delta Queen* and sister *Mississippi Queen* met to discuss the possibility of launching a "Delta Queen on rails."

"We were constantly approached by passengers who wondered why there wasn't a deluxe train in North America," Mueller recalled decades later. "We felt that the Americana cruise concept could be easily transferred to rails and open up America's treasures not touched by inland waterways. The Delta Queen Steamboat Company had a massive mailing list, an excellent reputation, and was flush with cash. We figured that a 1990 launch celebrating the 100th anniversary of the company's founding [as the Greene Line] might be appropriate."

Mueller was given the task of assembling this package, the "Grand American Railway" project. A year and a half later he delivered the proposal in two leather-bound albums to company executives. It called for a 150-passenger, all-suite, bi-level train to connect with the two riverboats at St. Louis and New Orleans. Possibly Amtrak's surplus ex–Santa Fe *El Capitan* cars could be rebuilt, or new cars could be created from scratch. But events redirected the company's priorities.

"In December of that year," according to Mueller, "the *Mississippi Queen* collided with a barge and nearly capsized, and the rail project was placed on the back burner in favor of the *Belle of America*." This luxurious new steamboat was given the name "American Queen," as it turned out—and, in another curious twist, was launched in 1995, the same year that *AOE* began land-cruise service from Washington to Sacramento, as well as the year that Mueller became the company's president.

Mueller and Zuger were actually the first passengers to ride *AEE*'s most illustrious car and new addition, the *New York* observation. After mechanical work was completed at Northern Rail Car, the car was fitted out at Panama City. It then deadheaded up to Washington, where the pair boarded for the quick ride up the Northeast Corridor to New York City. (From there the car would be forwarded to Chicago to join the *Greenbrier Limited* consist.) Zuger and Mueller batted around the cruise-train concept, along with possibilities for "rail and sail" options.

In any event, as a "land cruise" linked with the illustrious Greenbrier, *AEE* was now clearly on the right track, so to speak, and ridership began to build. Then, on June 21, in the fourth month of *Greenbrier Limited* service, the train went *off* the track—literally, south of Monon, Indiana, on CSX's former Louisville & Nashville line. A harvester that had "bottomed out" on a grade crossing and been abandoned by its driver derailed the locomotives (GP40-2's leased by *AEE* from National Railway Equipment to replace the CSX F's), the MARC F-unit trailing them to provide head-end power, and 7 of the 11 passenger cars, sparing only sleepers *Paris* and *Washington,* diner *Chicago,* and observation *New York.* Among the 16 crew and 31 passengers (which included many *AEE* stockholders), there was only one minor injury, a broken arm for a crew member. The cars were equipped with tightlock couplers, fortunately, so none turned over.

"The derailment was very traumatic," Mueller recalled, "even though we were back in service in ten days, albeit with a shorter train." Mueller recounted his reaction on first learning of the derailment.

"I was walking down the platform at the REA Building adjacent to Union Station in Washington, where we had offices," he said. "The station superintendent was Tom Chawluk, and when I passed his office he waved frantically through the glass for me to come in.

"As soon as I cleared the doorway he cupped the phone and said that the train was on the ground in Indiana. It was an agonizing wait until we learned that there had been no serious injuries or deaths. Then Bill Spann and the rest of the management team began making plans to move the train to Chicago and to let booked passengers know the next few trips would be cancelled. The heartbreaking thing was that load factors at that point were very high and holding." Specifically, the company reported that 7,394 passengers had ridden the train from March through June, 30 percent of these for business and the balance for leisure. With monthly operating costs of about $850,000, and monthly ticket sales typically exceeding $1 million, the train had been turning a profit.

Four cars were severely damaged (*Monte Carlo* was the worst), though none fatally, but replacements had to be leased while repairs were made, and even with these stand-ins more than $1 million in fares had to be refunded. John Kirkwood's four cars were used, along with a 10-roomette, 6–double bedroom sleeper—*Palm Leaf,* built by American Car & Foundry in 1951 for Santa Fe.

Still the train soldiered on, and plans were made and announced for the consist to shift to a New York-Miami run from November through March as *The Royal Floridian.* A tie-in with the Ocean Reef Club and Resort in Key Largo, 50 miles south of Miami, would emulate the Greenbrier connection. But monthly ticket sales had dwindled to $400,000 after the derailment, according to Spann. And bad luck continued to dog the *AEE.* When a press excursion for the Florida service killed two girls who were trespassing on Northeast Corridor tracks near Philadelphia, this no doubt further disquieted stockholders and potential investors.

So in mid-October of 1991, just under two years after its inauguration with much hoopla and high hopes, the *American-European Express* quietly died.

"I thought I had the little train that could," Bill Spann was quoted as saying. "And then all of a sudden someone pulled the rug out from under me." Though Spann had hopes of raising the funds needed to restart the service, a sum he estimated at $4 million, the train went into storage, taken initially to the CSX yards in Jacksonville. Eric Levin and Greg Mueller made the three-day, two-night trip with the train from Chicago to Jacksonville on the back of a 57-car CSX freight train.

"The sadness of the trip was tempered by the fact that we knew the train would not stay mothballed for long," Mueller recalled later, "and I knew that when it returned to service it would be in land-cruise format." Subsequent events have proved him prescient.

photo gallery

On December 31, 1990, the New Year's Eve special leaves Chicago Union Station. *Bruce C. Nelson.*

Bill and Melissa Spann celebrate on the *AEE*'s inaugural run—October 28, 1989. *Bob Johnston.*

Dining car *Zurich* looks elegant from within and without. *Karl Zimmermann.*

DINNER

Aboard the Dining Car Chicago
between
Washington, D.C. and New York, N.Y.
November 9, 1989

Duck Consomme
Julienne of Oriental Vegetables

———

Salad of Three Greens and Flowers
Herbal Vinaigrette

———

Poached Salmon
Cucumber Beurre Blanc
Caviar Garni

———

Sorbet of Pink Grapefruit

———

Veal Roulade with Game Force
Jus Mederia

Baby Vegetables   Turned Potatoes

———

A Selection of Fruits and Cheeses

———

Sacher Torte with Cognac Cream

———

Coffee and Tea Service

———

Wines
Kenwood '88 Sauvignon Blanc
Clos du Bois '86 Merlot

The menu for the November 9, 1989, trip for the press.
Karl Zimmermann Collection.

AEE's house champagne.
Bob Johnston.

ABOVE: On November 16, 1989, Oprah Winfrey brought some celebrity glamour to *AEE* when she did her show aboard. *Bob Johnston.*

In the *AEE* kitchen, Jeff Pawlak and William Stepek flank Executive Chef Art Smith. Smith would become Oprah's personal chef, a cookbook author, and a television personality. *Bob Johnston.*

Running as part of Amtrak's *Congressional*, the *AEE* is Washington-bound as it leaves the station in Wilmington. *Karl Zimmermann.*

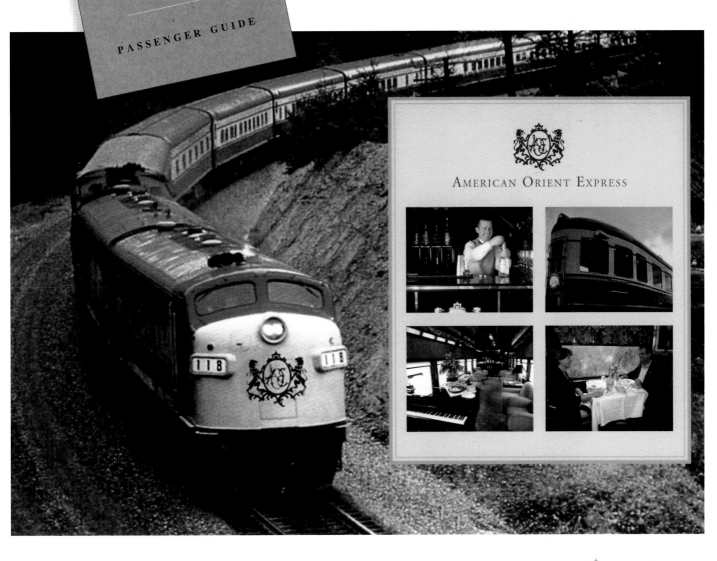

The *American-European Express* Passenger Guide carries a photograph of the train running as the Greenbrier Limited in the mountains of West Virginia. *Gregory Mueller Collection.*

BELOW: Airbrushed, this image was used for many years into the *American Orient Express* era, as on this postcard, though the train never operated with its own diesels, let alone streamlined ones. *Karl Zimmermann Collection.*

Running on its own, the *AEE* roars through Metropark, New Jersey. *Karl Zimmermann.*

In May of 1991, the *AEE* is westbound at Burke, Virginia, on Norfolk Southern behind GP-40-2 diesels leased from National Railway Equipment. *Alex Mayes.*

The "Heart of the South Limited" hustles north near Betts, Florida, on February 9, 1991, behind a pair of Bay Line GP38s. Sleepers *Montecito* and *Bella Vista,* leased from Rail Ventures, are at the head of the train. *Bruce C. Nelson.*

Club car *St. Moritz* and a Bay Line GP38 share space in Panama City's Sherman Yard on February 7, 1991. *Bruce C. Nelson.*

RIGHT: Brochures were published for the *Royal Floridian,* though the train never operated. *Gregory Mueller Collection.*

AMERICAN·EUROPEAN EXPRESS
RAILWAY TRAIN DELUXE

Winter Travel Plans
November 1991 – March 1992

The Royal Floridian

Serving

NEW YORK/PHILADELPHIA/WILMINGTON
BALTIMORE, WASHINGTON AND
ORLANDO, WEST PALM BEACH,
FORT LAUDERDALE, MIAMI AND THE
OCEAN REEF CLUB AND RESORT

Operated In Conjunction
With The Nostalgie
Istanbul Orient Express

AOE westbound in Colorado in October of 1998. *Karl Zimmermann.*

3

American Orient Express

THE PHOENIX RISES

In 1994, 11 extraordinary *American-European Express* cars were sitting idle on CSX property—in Jacksonville at first, but as of 1992 in the former Central of Georgia Yard in Atlanta. They had languished for close to three years, still and silent, aside from a few occasions when *AEE* creditor CSX used *New York* and some of the sleepers in its business trains. Though William Spann and his Swiss partners had hopes of getting the train back in service, these never panned out. For one thing, uncertainties in the European economy, especially in the transport sector, were having an impact on Intraflug and were a distraction from efforts to get *AEE* back on the rails. (In fact, Intraflug was bought out in 1992, and Zuger left and joined Reisebüro Mittelthurgau, a Swiss travel company more focused on tourism, taking the *NIOE* and *AEE* cars with him.)

Thus it took another entrepreneur, Texan George Pierce, to write the consist's next chapter, and the first under the name "American Orient Express." Pierce had served in the Texas House of Representatives and, more to the point, had been the majority stockholder of the *Texan Dinner Train,* which ran from San Antonio to Hondo, Texas. (Pierce sold the train in 1991 to Transcisco Tours, operator of the ill-fated *Sierra 49er Express;* Transcisco shut the dinner train down within a year.) Branson, Missouri, the country music center that sprung up in the Ozarks, proved to be the catalyst that energized the *American Orient Express.*

Branson caught Pierce's attention when he saw a feature on *60 Minutes* about the town's burgeoning popularity. He went to take a look for himself and, as he said, "fell in love with the place." While there, he noticed that the railroad tracks into town—the Missouri & Northern Arkansas—were in good shape and paralleled a scenic river for many miles. Out of the legislature and without his dinner train, he was, he said, "bored." Thinking that a train from his hometown of San Antonio to Branson might be a good idea, he started to hunt for rail cars. The trail led to Georgia, where the idle *AEE* was stored.

The next thing George Pierce knew, he was president and chief executive officer of the *American Orient Express*. The *AOE* in this first incarnation was a joint venture of Pierce's TransTexas Rail and Reisebüro Mittelthurgau, Edy Zuger's new company. In February 1994 the cars were moved to San Antonio, where they received some mechanical updates and remodeling—and a new name on the letterboards, "American Orient Express," with the gold-lined cream and blue livery otherwise remaining unchanged. In August of 1994 the *Branson Limited* operated for the first time, taking Missouri Pacific's historic *Eagle* route as far as Newport, Arkansas, and finishing on the M&NA from there to Branson. By year's end there were eight additional departures.

In 1995, the *AOE* ran eight more trips to Branson, along with three San Antonio-New Orleans excursions. The Branson trips were actually five-day packages that included a champagne reception, two nights on the train with meals, two hotel nights in Branson with breakfast and dinner, five shows, and transfers.

"The Branson trips were less successful than we had hoped," according to Kathy Eastman, who served for many years as *AOE*'s director of tour operations and, before that, as general manager of Pierce's dinner train. "Operating costs were higher than we'd initially projected, which pushed ticket prices too high for the Branson clientele." Casting about for other marketing ideas, Eastman approached Neiman Marcus, the Dallas-based department-store chain perhaps most famous for its Christmas catalogues featuring extravagant, larger-than-life, over-the-top gifts. This led to the "Neiman Marcus Holiday Express," which operated in the pre-Christmas seasons of 1994 and 1995, using basically the leased *AOE* train, and acted as a rolling retail store to bring Neiman Marcus shopping to cities where the company had no permanent outlets. The tour garnered a great deal of media attention wherever it went.

To supplement the *AOE*'s dozen cars, the retailer leased some Amtrak equipment as well: a diner, a baggage car, and a pair of F40PH diesels to haul the entire assemblage. Since diners *Zurich* and *Chicago,* club cars *St. Moritz* and *Bay Point Club,* and observation *New York* were to be used for merchandise display, most of their furnishings were carefully removed (the club cars' pianos couldn't be, of course) and stored in Neiman Marcus's warehouse in Dallas. The sleeping cars were used as originally intended, for sleeping—by the roughly 50 Neiman Marcus and 25 *AOE* personnel who staffed the train. They all took their meals in the Amtrak diner, since *AOE*'s diners were full of goods for sale.

The 1995 tour was more ambitious than the previous year's, visiting ten cities in 27 days, beginning November 19. Stops from one to three days in length were made at San Antonio, New Orleans, Jackson (Mississippi), Memphis, Nashville, Louisville, Cincinnati, Pittsburgh, Cleveland, and Indianapolis.

The five merchandise display cars were marshaled at the end of the train. Shoppers, who were required to reserve a time slot in advance by calling a toll-free number, would enter the forward car, walk through all the displays, and exit from the *New York* (where the high-ticket items like furs and jewelry were to be found). This car carried an attractive drumhead, which read "NM Holiday Special," encircled with the words "Neiman Marcus on the American Orient Express 1995." Though this special charter was judged highly successful, it was not repeated. It would prove to be George Pierce's swan song with the train.

The next player in the evolution of the *American Orient Express* was T. C. Swartz, and he was already on board, having collaborated with Pierce during the 1995 season. His Seattle-based TCS Expeditions is a travel company specializing in the unusual, offbeat, and upmarket. Edy Zuger had worked with him when Swartz had booked passengers on the *Nostalgie Istanbul Orient Express* and was able to interest him in the *AOE*. As a result, TCS Expeditions and TransTexas Rail Corporation ran four "Across the Continent" trips—eight nights, between Washington, D.C., and Sacramento—as a joint venture (with the train still in TransTexas lease) in 1995. There was also a New York City-San Francisco special charter for Swiss passengers, organized by Zuger. The following season, with Greg Mueller as president (he had been introduced to T. C. Swartz by Zuger), TCS Expeditions would be sole operator of the train.

"In September of 1995, to lay the foundation for the national parks trips we'd inaugurate the next season," recalls Mueller, who had just that month been appointed president, "T. C. Swartz and I met with Bob Lacivita, Grand Canyon Railway's vice-president and general manager, at the newly completed Fray Marcos Hotel in Williams, planning the frequencies and timings and turnarounds from Williams to the South Rim, while factoring in the mechanical needs for the consist. Then we called on Bob Sarr at Santa Fe Southern and made similar arrangements for the train to use the old ATSF line from Lamy right into the depot in downtown Santa Fe." That original Parks program would be a

2,200-mile, nine-night journey from Denver to Santa Fe via Salt Lake City, Zion National Park, and the Grand Canyon, and included Rocky Mountain National Park for a pre-trip overnight (a feature dropped after one year).

The following month, Swartz, Mueller, and Zuger met at Amtrak headquarters in Washington Union Station with Amtrak officials to nail down the operating agreement for the 1996 season. Amtrak agreed to provide motive power, crews, station services, and access to its entire system, and numerous short lines in addition, via a single contract, an arrangement that in essence has been in place ever since.

"All through the winter of 1995–1996 we continued to plan for the first full season of the land-cruise operation," Mueller explained, "which was much more complex than running a train between two endpoints." In addition to the "National Parks of the West" itineraries, *AOE* in 1996 would offer "The Great Transcontinental Journey" (eight nights between Washington, D.C., and Los Angeles) and "The Rockies & Sierras," a five-night trip between Denver and Oakland that included stops at Salt Lake City, Lake Tahoe (with the train actually parked at Truckee), and Napa Valley. Pre- and post-trip overnights for that year were at San Francisco's Huntington Hotel on Nob Hill and Rocky Mountain National Park.

"We had to tackle provisioning, staffing, and ground services at remote locations and intermediate stops," Mueller continued. "We had to obtain approval from the carriers for travel off the Amtrak network. It was the hardest single thing I have ever done in aviation, maritime, or rail." That winter, two new crew cars were acquired, and major renovations were made to the train's sleepers (primarily the addition of more Presidential Suites) and club cars. (Details of these acquisitions and changes can be found in chapter 5.)

The image of CSX's ex-Clinchfield F-units—photographed in the mountains of Appalachia on the point of the *Greenbrier Limited* and later airbrushed into *AOE* dress—would turn up on *AOE* postcards for many years, and folk-art versions of streamlined, bulldog-nosed diesels with the *AOE* logo would be used on company catalogues as late as the 2002–2003 edition. The operating reality, however, is that the company has never had its own diesels. Amtrak units have hauled the *American Orient Express* right from the beginning, assisted by Canadian National units on Canadian itineraries and Ferrocarril Mexicano freight locomotives (with a leased Amtrak F40PH trailing along just to supply head-end power) when the train ran in Mexico. Electro-Motive Division's F40PH's and General Electric's P32's (which wore the "Pepsi-can" paint scheme) shared the honors until late 1997, when GE's "Genesis" P40's and P42's took over.

Whatever the power, operations were not always routine. In April of 1996, for instance, during the first season of offering "The Great Transcontinental Journey" between Washington, D.C., and Los Angeles, on the southern route, passengers detrained in New Orleans right after breakfast for their tour. As the train pulled away from the platform to head for the mechanical facility west of the station, one section of rail turned on its side and nine cars were dragged off the track. Coming in mid-trip as it did, this could have been a major crisis—even a trip-ending one. But *AOE*'s on-board mechanics and the New Orleans Amtrak team were able to inspect the train, do a wheel inventory, and make replacements and repairs in time for a midnight departure—only six hours late. This quick turnaround saved the company hundreds of thousands of dollars.

The 1997 season was more ambitious yet, with a number of new itineraries: "The Great Trans-Canada Rail Journey" (eight nights, between Montreal and Vancouver), "The Great Northwest" (five nights, between Portland and Kalispell, Montana), "The Rockies & Yellowstone" (five nights, between Portland and Salt Lake City), and "The Great Southwest" (four nights from Los Angeles to Santa Fe, operated just once). One lesson learned was that the early itineraries included too many rail miles per day—bad for the balance sheet, for one thing, and arguably not what most passengers wanted anyway.

Readying the train for the first-ever "Great Trans-Canada Rail Journey" required a positioning move from Denver (at the conclusion of a "National Parks of the West" trip) to Seattle and north into Canada. Rather than run empty as a deadhead, *AOE* seized the opportunity to host officials from Amtrak and VIA Rail Canada, as well as various railroads—as both a way to say "thank you" for past and future cooperation and an opportunity to brainstorm for upcoming seasons. The trip was very successful, with representatives aboard from Norfolk Southern, CSX, Union Pacific, Santa Fe, Canadian Pacific, and Canadian National.

The next step in the evolution of the *American Orient Express* came in late 1997 with the train's purchase by Henry Hillman, who would become chairman, CEO and, after Mueller's resignation in April of 1998, president of the company.

"The idea came to me in 1994 aboard a Seabourn ship, on a cruise to Normandy marking the anniversary of the invasion," says Hillman, who for 20 years had been an entrepreneur in venture capital. (A member of the wealthy Pittsburgh steel family, Hillman has been an active philanthropist as well.) "My wife and I had a great time on this luxurious ship, and it got me to thinking that I'd love to see the Grand Canyon or Yellowstone—lots of places in the United States—in this same style.

"I wouldn't consider myself a rail buff—except that we're all railfans at heart. As a kid, I rode trains everywhere, and had a train set. But in time I joined that vast majority of Americans who, according to surveys, like trains but never ride them. I hadn't been on a long-distance train in a dozen years, but now I rode a few—and kept my eye on the market." Hillman sampled Amtrak's *Coast Starlight, Empire Builder,* and *Auto Train;* the *Rocky Mountaineer* in Canada; and the *American Orient Express.*

This led to Hillman's acquisition—on November 14, 1997—of the *AOE* operation from TCS Expeditions, and the purchase of the equipment from Reisebüro Mittelthurgau. For the 1998 season, TCS Expeditions continued to handle the booking, but Hillman's people took over on-board services. The operations center for *AOE* was established in Denver. Public relations, marketing, and sales were run from Downers Grove, Illinois (under the direction of Peter Boese, at first vice-president of sales and marketing, later executive vice-president, and finally president), while Oregon Rail Holdings, the business end of the operations, and Hillman himself were located in Portland, Oregon. On-board services, tour management, and the like were based in the Denver office on Wynkoop, across the street from Union Station. Car maintenance and refurbishing was done for a time in the Denver suburb of Englewood, in a facility once owned by General Iron Works. With three overhead cranes, two of 50-ton capacity, this space could accommodate a dozen cars indoors.

Expansion was on Hillman's mind from the start, and in June of 1999 he would acquire the American West Steamboat Company, whose sternwheeler *Queen of the West* made week-long sailings on the Columbia, Snake, and Willamette rivers.

"We think it fits very well with the other operations of our company," Hillman said when he took over American West. "Down the road, we'll be looking at rail-cruise packages." This never happened, though in 2003 a second vessel, the *Empress of the North,* joined the fleet. This boat was designed to spend summers cruising up the Inside Passage to Alaska while joining the *Queen of the West* on the Columbia River and tributaries for the balance of the year. American West Steamboat did appear in *AOE* brochures, and vice versa.

In 1998, the year before acquiring American West Steamboat, Hillman bought Montana Rockies Rail Tours, operator of the *Montana Daylight.* This excursion train had been in business since 1995 over Montana Rail Link between Sandpoint in Idaho (with bus transfer from Spokane) and Livingston in Montana (with bus transfer to Billings or Bozeman). This was a two-day trip with an off-train overnight stay in Missoula, Montana; motor coach extensions were available to Yellowstone and Grand Teton national parks or Glacier National Park.

John Kirkwood, who later would be asked to join the *AOE* board to provide railroading expertise, and whose cars had been leased by *AEE* right from the beginning of its operations, was the founder, chairman, and president of MRRT, for which he provided the principal financing.

"Amtrak cutbacks in the early 1990s hurt the rail charter business," he would explain years later. "My company, Rail Ventures, had deluxe cars with very little place to run them." Ken Keeler in Portland was renovating equipment for Kirkwood. Rail Ventures' cars were used on a special birthday train for Dennis Washington, president of Montana Rail Link. Connections were made, and *Montana Daylight* was born.

Unlike the all-luxury *AOE,* the *Montana Daylight* provided three levels of service. "Big Sky" offered dome cars and "gourmet lunches" served on linen and china aboard dining car *Missouri River,* while "Explorer" passengers rode in reclining seat "flat-top" coaches and ate deli-style box lunches. "Gold Nugget," the third option, available to groups of four or more passengers only, was tantamount to chartering a private car: open-platform *Yerba Buena* augmented by Rail Ventures' other cars.

Marcia Pilgeram—who, like Keeler, would be involved in the operation all the way through—came in to run the on-train operations. They started with just five trips in 1995, then eight the following year.

"We were still underfinanced," Kirkwood says, a problem that continued through the 1998 season. At the end of it, he sold the operation to Hillman.

"We were looking for a bigger marketing operation than we could afford," according to Kirkwood, "and we knew Henry Hillman could provide that." Though Hillman's Oregon Rail Holdings had bought Montana Rockies Rail Tours after its 1998 season, the *Montana Daylight* would run the following year just as in the past, but using some equipment, including an ex-Amtrak buffet-lounge, newly acquired by Hillman. The operation continued to be managed out of Sandpoint with existing (though supplemented) staff. For the 2000 season, however, there were big plans. Renamed "American Spirit," the Montana run was to be joined by a similarly equipped Portland-Whitefish train over Burlington Northern Santa Fe, using some of the *Montana Daylight*'s equipment and some newly acquired cars. Like the *AOE*, this new service would be operated by Amtrak, with Amtrak power.

Hillman's vision and the reality of this expansion turned out to be worlds apart. The projected ten-car consist of the new train was to include a baggage car, crew car (*Swift Stream,* former New York Central 6–double bedroom, buffet-lounge), two coaches, buffet-lounge, diner, three dome coaches (including *Silver Scene,* from Chicago, Burlington & Quincy's 1947 *Twin Zephyr*), and a dome. The *Montana Daylight* consist was to be similar. Both trains would run under the name "American Spirit."

As matters played out, little of this expansion actually happened. Problems abounded with the Portland-Whitefish leg. Few additional cars were ever refurbished, and the Amtrak cars leased as stand-ins were poorly received by passengers. Many trips were canceled altogether. At the end of the season, Hillman sold Montana Rockies Rail Tours to RailQuest America, a group of employees and investors led once again by Kirkwood.

"I decided that we could step back in," Kirkwood said, "fool that I was." In fact, this was not an unreasonable assumption, since the Montana leg had continued to do well, even while the Portland train fizzled. Pilgeram, who had born the brunt of the previous season's customer dissatisfaction, became president and CEO, while Keller was vice-president, and Kirkwood chair.

One innovation of the reborn *Montana Daylight* was "Montana Gold," a high-end option that was an evolution of the earlier "Gold Nugget." The cars for this, recently acquired by Kirkwood's Rail Ventures, were sleeper *Gallatin River* and *Glacier Park,* a dome car with open observation platform that had been rebuilt to private-car configuration—and that would turn up as the tail car on *AOE I* for the 2003 season.

Unhappily, after all these ups and downs, Montana Rockies Rail Tours was forced to throw in the towel after the 2004 season. They shut down and sold their equipment, most of it to a California railway-car broker. The dome cars went to Alaska, and that chapter of the Oregon Rail Holdings story was definitively closed.

In late 1998, when Hillman purchased *Montana Daylight,* other projects were on the docket also, if further out. *AOE* had acquired former Milwaukee Road Super Dome No. 58 and, subsequently, a pair of ex–Union Pacific domes—a coach and a lounge, both to be refurbished as lounges. While the Milwaukee dome's eventual deployment was never certainly set, firm plans were laid for the UP cars to join the *AOE* consist in 2001. The under-dome cocktail room might have been converted to passenger services office and gift shop, allowing lounge *Seattle* (which then housed the office) to drop out of the consist at times. In fact, these UP cars never were refurbished, but exactly the same use projected for their under-dome space was made of the lower level of the ex–Great Northern *Empire Builder* domes that *AOE* would buy from Amtrak in 2002.

The ex-Milwaukee or ex-UP cars would have helped meet Hillman's first objective as the *AOE* operation expanded—to have adequate equipment to operate the train year-round by rotating cars out piecemeal for maintenance, rather than bringing the entire consist in at once (and thus losing months from the operating schedule). Once the two UP domes were refurbished, his thinking went, the train would run with one dome and either the *Seattle* or the *Rocky Mountain*. These cars would also be a step toward the second objective: two complete consists on the road. This is what eventually happened, but with the ex–*Empire Builder* "Great Domes"—in good shape, and already equipped for head-end-power operations when acquired from Amtrak. They would be key cars in the inauguration of *AOE II* when it finally hit the rails in 2002.

From 1996, the year that, under the banner of TCS Expeditions, the *American Orient Express* adopted what is essentially GrandLuxe Rail's current modus operandi, itineraries have been in a constant (if often gentle) state of flux. Some have been tried and have failed, for lack of bookings. One, "The Orange Blossom Explorer," appeared in the brochure but never actually ran, again a victim of too few bookings and, possibly, tardy promotion. Others have become standbys, though even these perennial favorites have been tweaked from year to year.

For 1998, the first season under Hillman ownership, the itineraries had been planned and advertised by TCS Expeditions. One itinerary was dropped—"The Great Southwest," for which only a single departure had been actually operated the previous year—and three added. One of these, "The Antebellum South," six nights between Washington, D.C., and New Orleans, became an early-spring perennial, finally spoiled in 2006 in the aftermath of Hurricane Katrina (when the trip ran only as far south as Savannah, eschewing New Orleans) and discontinued entirely for 2007. Another, the four-night Chicago-to-New Orleans "Jazz and Blues Express," operated only twice that year and was dropped after one more season; one problem, apparently, was that poor track conditions caused the train to run unacceptably late. The third new offering,

"American Heritage," a nine-night trip from Montreal to Washington, D.C., via Boston and New England, ran its one scheduled departure and was gone the next season. (It was, however, a precursor of "Autumn in New England & Quebec," which would be offered four years later.)

In 1999, then, the *AOE* offered nine itineraries, ranging from five to ten days in length: "Jazz and Blues Express," "Antebellum South," "Pacific Coast Explorer," "Great Transcontinental Journey," "National Parks of the West," "Rockies and Yellowstone," "Great Northwest," "Trans-Canada Rail Journey," and "Quebec and the Canadian Maritimes." As always, the itineraries involved plentiful stops along the way for tours by motor coach to area sights; most overnights were aboard the train, though some tours included hotel stays.

The nine-day "National Parks" trip, for instance, began with an overnight aboard in Denver before the train headed for Salt Lake City via the ex–Denver & Rio Grande Western Moffat Tunnel route. From there it continued southwest on the Union Pacific, dropping passengers for a coach tour of Bryce and Zion, with a hotel overnight. At Barstow the train turned east on Santa Fe rails, detouring from Williams to the South Rim on the Grand Canyon Railway. The tour ended with the slow jog up the 18-mile Santa Fe Southern from Lamy, New Mexico, to Santa Fe that had been arranged by Swartz and Mueller.

In his early years at its helm, Hillman had been pleased with the AOE as it was evolving. "It's running beautifully," he said in late 1999, "generally at full occupancy. We'll continue to refine the operation, but I don't see any major changes.

"Our train has all the advantages of a cruise ship," he continued. "My father, who's 80, would never have seen the Grand Canyon, or Bryce and Zion, without the *AOE*. He wants a higher quality than Denny's and Best Western. That's our clientele—someone who's well-traveled and would like to see the U.S. in a luxury kind of way."

In the early years of his ownership, Hillman was very much the hands-on manager, interesting himself in all aspects of the operation. By October of 2003, however, when he appointed Peter Boese president of *AOE,* he had drifted away. At about that time he resigned as CEO and chairman of the board, leaving Boese thoroughly in charge. Boese had, in fact, been central to the company from the beginning, Hillman's trusted lieutenant; the location of the sales and marketing office in Downers Grove had been at his behest.

Whether under Henry Hillman or Peter Boese's direction, the central core of itineraries remained stable through the years that the train was owned by Oregon Rail Holdings. "National Parks of the West," boosted by a widely viewed PBS travelogue, became the stellar performer. The "Pacific Coast Explorer," which in 2004 and afterward acquired a culinary emphasis, became another standby, as did the Canadian and southern United States transcontinentals. The U.S. trip, never offered more than three times a season and as few as one, was used in part to reposition the train to or from "Antebellum South" (another regular trip, sometimes marketed with a Civil War or jazz theme) or from "Autumn in New England and Quebec" (after it was added in 2002) to Los Angeles to begin "Pacific Coast Explorer" trips. One projected trip, the brainchild of Neil Wright, *AOE*'s director of transportation for many years, was a complicated itinerary wending its way from Richmond to St. Louis and through Montana in celebration of the Lewis and Clark bicentennial. Popular Lewis and Clark historian Stephen Ambrose would have been an on-board lecturer, but the ambitious routing finally proved just too difficult to organize.

The big change came with the addition of a second train, *AOE II,* announced in the brochure for the 2002 season but in the works for some years.

"The concept," as Henry Hillman explained it early in 2002, "is to divide the *AOE* into two separate consists—essentially indistinguishable in service and accommodations, though I can't replicate the *New York* car." The motivation behind it? "We aren't able to offer the number of trips with one consist that our passengers want. We have a waiting list of over 1,500 for the trans-Canada trip. We'll add that and more of the 'National Parks' trips as well." From the beginning, in fact, all principals saw that more capacity, however realized, would be the key to financial success.

However, getting the second train into service proved problematic in the extreme.

The plan had been for one train to begin the year on February 19 with a U.S. transcontinental, spend March and April doing "Antebellum South" runs, and May offering three more "transcons." Both trains would do "Pacific Coast Explorer" runs, then one would head north to spend June through August making trans-Canada trips, followed in September and October by a new, Boston-based itinerary: "Autumn in New England & Quebec." Then one more "Great Transcontinental Rail Journey" and "Pacific Coast Explorer" would bring it home to Western Junction, near Tenino, Washington. There, in late 2001, *AOE* had relocated its shops in a small facility leased from Tacoma Rail, a railway unique in being part of a public utility. Meanwhile, the other train would spend the season doing national parks and North-west itineraries.

This plan was predicated on having *American Orient Express II* ready to roll in May 2002—which it wasn't. Work continued apace in Tenino on the two ex–Great Northern domes and sleepers *Santa Fe* and *Montreal,* and at Colorado Railcar's Fort Lupton facility on *Charleston* and *Bar Harbor.* Sleeper-lounge *Swift Stream,* originally acquired for the *American Spirit,* was pulled out of mothballs for use as a crew sleeper. The search was on for additional suitable feature cars (in addition to the splendid domes) and turned up a twin-unit diner acquired from BC Rail that became *Jasper* and *Vancouver* and, on lease for the season, an ex–*California Zephyr* dome observation to assume the unenviable role of being *New York*'s counterpart. However, this didn't all come together until September, when *AOE II* made its debut.

The train's troubles were not over, though, since the "Autumn in New England & Quebec" itinerary as first conceived had some inherent problems. Originating in Boston, the trip was to begin with a quick sprint down Amtrak's electrified Northeast Corridor to New London, where the train would head north on the ex–Central Vermont route (now New England Central Railroad, part of RailAmerica). Because the dome car was barred from operating under catenary, it had to be added or subtracted at New London, and the power changed there as well; both operations were time-consuming. But the real problem came from the four border crossings in and out of Canada that the itinerary required, some in the middle of the night, a serious inconvenience for passengers. (The following year the trip was switched to Montreal-based from Boston-based and ran far more smoothly.)

The other new itinerary announced in the 2002 brochure, though not actually operated until January 2003, was "The Southwest & Mexico's Copper Canyon," which would run between Tucson (boarding the train at Magdalena, not far over the border into Mexico) to Juarez (for El Paso) via the scenically spectacular Copper Canyon region. The itinerary proved popular and ran successfully through the 2003 season and the next, on essentially the same route but now called "Copper Canyon & Colonial Mexico."

The 2005 Copper Canyon season started out fine too, but on February 23, the first evening of that year's fourth trip, things took a nasty turn. With the train running south about two hours out of Nogales (which the year before had replaced Magdalena as the western boarding point), most passengers were in diners *Zurich* and *Chicago* after the "welcome aboard" reception. Then, as one passenger reported, "everything began shaking violently. The car was bouncing up and down, hard, and rocking side to side." Though the train was traveling at only 18 miles per hour on Ferrocarril Mexicano's rough track, most of the cars derailed: the front four sleepers, piano lounge, two diners, and dome. Happily, there was only one minor injury, to a member of the kitchen staff.

Passengers were led back to the four rear sleepers and observation, which had remained on the track. There those with rooms in the derailed cars sat in the *New York* or shared space with the incumbent passengers while the porters packed up their belongings, since passengers were not allowed to re-enter the derailed cars. Hours passed before a Ferrocarril Mexicano (Ferromex) diesel arrived to pull the five cars still on the track back toward Nogales. At about 3 AM the truncated train reached a grade crossing, where a bus met it to take the displaced passengers to the hotel in Tucson where they'd begun the trip. The orphaned cars then lumbered on to Nogales, those passengers from the last four sleepers, with their rooms once again their own, catching a few hours' sleep before disembarking. Though none of the cars were seriously or permanently damaged, some upcoming trips had to be cancelled.

Mexico wasn't finished with its devilment, either. For the 2006 season, management decided to operate the Mexico trips, scheduled to begin January 28, as an out-and-back itinerary from Juarez, rather than the U-shaped one-way of earlier years. The fall 2005 trips were switched to that itinerary as well. But in October, uncomfortable with the reports from the independent consultants they'd sent to evaluate track conditions on *that* route and certify its safety, and perhaps also by the liability situation they'd created by sending them, management decided to cancel all Mexico trips, filling in at the last minute with additional "Rockies & Sierras" departures for the fall and "Antebellum South" trips for late winter. Then Katrina blew in and caused that itinerary to be pulled back to Washington-Savannah only, diminishing its attractiveness.

The 2002 season, when the Mexican itinerary was first announced, also marked the loss, which happily proved temporary, of the ride that arguably was *AOE*'s most scenic: the run through Colorado on the former Denver & Rio Grande Western, the route of the *California Zephyr*. Apparently *AOE* management did some horse trading with Union Pacific, current operator of that line and no fan of passenger trains, either *AOE* or Amtrak. Citing traffic congestion on that single-track route (exacerbated by the need to exhaust diesel fumes from 6.21-mile

FACING PAGE: East of Crestmont in August of 1997, the *American Orient Express* is about to enter Tunnel #17. *Joe McMillan.*

Moffat Tunnel between train passages), UP wanted *AOE* off the line, and reportedly made some concessions elsewhere in exchange. The train would be back on that gloriously scenic line along the Colorado River beginning in 2005 with the "Rockies & Sierras" itinerary.

As all this was happening, with Henry Hillman out of the picture and the board serving as executive committee to run the train, a kind of stasis set in. Emphasis turned to economizing and keeping the train afloat until the next chapter could unfold. In January of 2006, the Hillman interests sold American West Steamboat to Ambassador Cruise Group, a division of Ambassadors International, which not long afterwards bought the Delta Queen Steamboat Company and renamed both companies Majestic America Line.

That left the Oregon Rail Holdings with just the *American Orient Express*—and that not for long.

photo gallery

The "Neiman Marcus Holiday Express" is at Riverside Park in Nashville. *Ralcon Wagner.*

ABOVE: Two classic observation cars—one of VIA Rail Canada's "Park" cars and *New York*—rub shoulders at Capreol, Ontario, when westbound *Canadian* pulls in next to the *AOE* in July of 2002. *Karl Zimmermann.*

Sleeper *Vienna* is one of the original *AEE* cars. *Karl Zimmermann.*

PREVIOUS PAGES: In July of 1997, the *AOE* plunges into Tunnel #13 west of Plain, Colorado. *Joe McMillan.*

Amtrak's Genesis diesels, in mismatched paint schemes, the older leading, power a 16-car *AOE* westbound at Rocky, Colorado, in October 1999. *Joe McMillan.*

ABOVE: In October of 1998, the *AOE* meets Amtrak's eastbound *California Zephyr* along the Colorado River. The *CZ* is carrying a trio of private cars. *Karl Zimmermann.*

Red markers and blue tailsign glow as the *New York* is ready for departure from Denver Union Station on November 2, 1998. *Chip Sherman.*

AMERICAN ORIENT EXPRESS

National Parks of the West
Sunday, October 18, 1998

Appetizer
Clam Chowder "New England Style"
Boston and Maine Railway
******

Chef's Specials
Venison with Cranberry Port Sauce
Canadian Pacific Railway

Pan Fried Catfish with Beurre Noisette
American Orient Express

Beef Tenderloin "Canadian Pacific Style"
Canadian Pacific Railway

Chicken with Dijon Cream Sauce
American Orient Express

Salmon Poached in Red Wine with Beurre Rouge
American Orient Express
******

Accompanied by
Orzo Gratinee
and
Baby Carrots
******

Pastry
Pumpkin Crème Brulee

ABOVE: This postcard shows off the *American Orient Express* at its best. *Karl Zimmermann Collection.*

In 1998, the dinner offerings were relatively limited, three courses rather than the later five, and entrees were attributed to various railroads. *Karl Zimmermann Collection.*

In September of 2002, the *AOE* races westbound along the Northeast Corridor near Mystic, Connecticut. The *New York* observation is leading since—a few miles ahead, at New London—the train will reverse direction as it turns north on the New England Central Railroad. *Karl Zimmermann.*

This ex–Great Northern dome car, repainted for the ill-fated
American Spirit, saw service as an *AOE* tail car in 2004.
Karl Zimmermann.

FACING PAGE: In February of 2005, Ferromex
diesels (with an Amtrak F40PH trailing to
provide head-end power) led the *AOE* past
the *Sierra Madre Express* at Bahuichivo on
the "Copper Canyon & Colonial Mexico"
itinerary. Trouble lies not far in the future.
Karl Zimmermann.

The bartender in the lounge
presents hors d'oeuvres.
Robert D. Turner.

The tables are set for dinner in the diner. *Robert D. Turner.*

4

The Old Order Changeth
GRANDLUXE RAIL JOURNEYS

When, on May 30, 2006, the news broke formally that the *American Orient Express*—which just a month earlier had been rebranded GrandeLuxe Rail Journeys—had been sold by Oregon Rail Holdings, it came as no great surprise. The sale had been long rumored and had in fact been five months in gestation. It was more a matter of waiting for the other shoe to drop, which it finally did on May 18—or 19, technically, in the wee hours.

The rumors had included the name of the purchaser: Thomas G. Rader, founder of Colorado Railcar Manufacturing, and before that Rader Railcar. For the record, the newly named GrandLuxe Rail Journeys was acquired by GrandLuxe Holdings, LLC, of which Tom Rader is chairman. John L. Thompson is president and Thomas E. Janaky vice president, sales; Thompson and Janaky both have been involved for many years with Colorado Railcar and other Rader interests.

GrandLuxe may have seemed an odd marriage, carbuilding and tour train operation, but in fact Rader had linked them more than two decades earlier, when he founded Tour Alaska, in 1982, with his wife, Ann, to provide the first private dome-car service in Alaska. Beyond that, he had actually begun his career in tourism—with Sheraton Hotels in Hawaii and then, from 1978 to 1982, as vice-president and general manager of cruise tours for Holland America Line/Westours.

For his Tour Alaska project, Rader had located five Milwaukee Road full-length domes, which had been built in 1952 by Pullman-Standard for use on the *Hiawatha*s. Of these cars, rounded up from various locations in the United States and Canada, one was scrapped immediately for parts (two 40-foot containers' worth), and three ultimately were restored: stripped, rewired, trucks rebuilt, new glass. Forty subcontractors did the work at the American Car & Foundry shops in Renton, Washington. The interiors were totally restyled, by Shirley La Follette, a noted designer from Seattle.

"We chose these Pullman-Standard cars," Rader recalled, "because they had bigger windows, were roomier, and had lower step-ups to the seating than the Budd-built full-length domes."

With these cars, which began operating in 1983 as the *Midnight Sun Express* attached to a regular-service Alaska Railroad train, Rader collected passengers from Cunard Line's cruise ships calling at Anchorage and took them to Denali National Park's Mount McKinley and Fairbanks. His service allowed them to continue their tour at a level of luxury commensurate to what they'd been enjoying on shipboard. The following year Holland America Line and Princess Cruises signed on with Tour Alaska as well.

By 1986, when Rader sold the operation to Princess Cruises and Princess Tours, annual sales had reached $29 million. He moved on from there. Beginning in 1988, Rader-built "Ultra Domes"—financed with the proceeds from the Tour Alaska sale—would replace those second-hand full-length domes with which Rader had started the Alaska operation on Princess's *Midnight Sun Express*. The first six Ultra Domes were created in the cut-down shells of ex–Southern Pacific San Francisco commute coaches acquired from Caltran, while all the others—and there would be many, since these Ultra Domes would become Rader's signature cars—were created from whole cloth. All are under glass every inch, from stem to stern (unlike earlier domes); on the lower level are luxurious dining facilities, typically for 36, and, on many of the cars, spacious open platforms for fresh-air sightseeing. The early Ultra Domes were built in a massive wooden building in Tillamook, Oregon, that had been a blimp hanger; seeking better rail access, more sunshine, and facilities available for rent, Rader Railcar operations were moved to Denver in January 1990.

By 1999 Princess Tours would have ten of these Ultra Domes operating as the *Midnight Sun Express* (they'd sell the ex-Milwaukee domes to Amtrak for its *Auto Train* after running them briefly as its own *California Sun Express*). Soon the other cruise lines would come knocking at Rader's door. Quietly, in 1986, Holland America had begun buying up all the full-length domes available, mostly cars built by the Budd Company for Santa Fe's *Chiefs*, hoping to corner the market. (They'd eventually get those same ex-Milwaukee domes from Amtrak as well, bringing them back to Alaska. Two are now owned by the Canon City & Royal Gorge Railroad.) With these cars, HAL/Westours began operating their *McKinley Explorer,* which, beginning in 2003, would itself be adding Ultra Domes to its operations—ten in all by 2005.

Celebrity Cruises and Royal Caribbean International were already on board by 2005, with their jointly operated *Wilderness Express,* using four cars delivered by Colorado Railcar in 2001 and 2002. Not to be outdone, host Alaska Railroad, which hauled all this bevy of Ultra Domes for the cruise lines, bought four of its own from 2005 to 2007—slightly different from the earlier domes in having the open observation area on the upper level. Similar Ultra Domes, 16 all told, provide the *Rocky Mountaineer*'s high-end "Gold Leaf" service, which operated first between Calgary and Banff and Vancouver, with service added subsequently between Jasper and Vancouver and, in 2006, between Jasper and Whistler on the former BC Rail route. The *Rocky Mountaineer* had received its first Ultra Domes in 1995, making it the second earliest operator after Princess.

Over the nearly two decades that Rader has been producing Ultra Domes, small refinements have ensued, but all 44 cars have much in common—most notably the huge amount of glass they carry, totally embracing the upper level to provide unobstructed viewing for all passengers. The curved panels (on most cars) are six feet by six feet; five inner layers of reflective and tinted inner material reduce solar gain by 62 percent. (The first ten of *Rocky Mountaineer*'s cars have smaller glass panels, one aligning with each dome seat for better visibility.) Four independent ten-ton air-conditioning units do the rest to eliminate what always had been a problem for dome cars: They were often too darn hot. Beyond comfort and attractive aesthetics, the Ultra Domes have another advantage that Rader stressed to woo customers, and that is economy. By his figuring, they have 39 percent more usable floor space than Amtrak's Superliners and 57 percent more than the full-length domes Budd and Pullman-Standard built for Santa Fe, Great Northern, and Milwaukee Road in the 1950s.

Rader has also built some single-level dome cars, most of which relate to a difficult aspect of the Rader Railcar and Colorado Railcar story. Operated by First American Railways of Hollywood, California, the *Florida Fun Train,* meant to be an amalgam of entertainment and tourism-based transportation connecting the beach destinations of south Florida with the theme parks of the Orlando area, began its short and troubled life in October 1997 with a consist that included three Rader Railcar–built single-level domes called "guest cars" (from among four coaches and a lounge with an open platform, actually an earlier prototype designed by Rader that had been on hold because of liability concerns). Also included were two bi-level "entertainment cars," one for children and one for adults; the latter included a dance floor and a Polynesian-themed "Tiki Rail Bar." Rader created these two cars within the shells of Chicago & North Western bi-level commuter coaches.

At the same time that the *Florida Fun Train* order was being completed, another substantial (and equally unusual) train was in progress at Rader Railcar: the 18-car *Marlboro Unlimited,* which was to host winners of a contest sponsored by Phillip Morris and had been six years in research and planning. This train was to break new ground in many ways. Though Amtrak's Superliners offered bi-level sleepers, the Marlboro train would have the first cars in America with beds actually in the dome area. (Europe's CityNightLine trains, which serve Switzerland, Germany, Austria, and the Netherlands, had introduced something close to that in 1995. They offer deluxe upper-level sleeping compartments with some overhead glass, though far less dramatic than the walls and ceiling of glass that was projected for the *Marlboro Unlimited* and, if all goes well, will now grace the *GrandLuxe Express.*)

Also unprecedented would be the mezzanine lounge car, with a lower-level dance floor in the center and an upper-level domed bar and lounge that overlooks it. There would be a tail car with a hot tub and open observation platform. The Marlboro cars were on the construction floor at Rader Railcar in Denver while, at Rader Railcar II in Fort Lupton, some 20 miles away, work proceeded on the *Florida Fun Train* and Ultra Domes for Princess Cruises and *Rocky Mountaineer.* This second facility had been opened to meet the construction demands of having the Ultra Domes, the *Florida Fun Train,* and the *Marlboro Unlimited* all in house on short deadlines at the same time.

Unfortunately, both these latter projects hit heavy seas. With the cars about 65 percent completed, for corporate reasons never completely made public, but thought to involve changing government regulations regarding ways tobacco companies may advertise, Philip Morris cancelled the *Marlboro Unlimited* project. Meanwhile, the *Florida Fun Train* was running 80 percent below projected capacity. (The operation would shut down in September 1998.) Hit from both sides, Rader Railcar chose, as Tom Rader later explained, "to reorganize in November 1997 under the Colorado Railcar name to protect our customers' interests while First American Railways went through bankruptcy proceedings." Rader's Denver facility and much of its contents were sold at auction.

Good times lay ahead, however. Nicely symbolic of that are the *Florida Fun Train*'s five single-level domes and its two entertainment cars, bought at bankruptcy auction in July 1999 by the Alaska Railroad.

THE COMPETITION
Successes and Failures

It seems so simple. Tap into Americans' seemly inexhaustible nostalgia for passenger trains—or at least their vision of what passenger trains were and are. Fix up some existing cars that no one else much wants. Run trains on tracks that are already there. Charge what seem like comfortably high prices. And, voila!

Failure.

More times than not over the last two decades, private operators of luxury and other recreational long-distance trains have been lured by that scenario and come up empty. It's far easier to count the successes than the failures: in addition to the *American Orient Express*, really just three in North America: the *Sierra Madre Express* in Mexico and the *Rocky Mountaineer* and *Royal Canadian Pacific* in Canada. (This count excludes the highly successful *Midnight Sun Express*, *McKinley Explorer*, and *Wilderness Express*, which run in Alaska as extensions of cruise-ship itineraries with Ultra Domes built by *Grand-Luxe* head Tom Rader. It also excludes such overseas successes as the *Venice Simplon-Orient-Express* and South Africa's *Pride of Africa*, operated by Rohan Vos's Rovas Rail.)

The last named of these three North American winners is the most anomalous and perhaps the most easily explained. The *Royal Canadian Pacific* is unique in that it's operated by a Class 1 railroad itself—which, for one thing, eliminates the conflicts with hosting freight railroads that sometimes trouble the *GrandLuxe* and other guest trains. The per diem fares are very substantial, one reason the train is successful. Another is that Canadian Pacific Railway doesn't require the *Royal Canadian Pacific*'s relatively few public trips to be a stand-alone profit center. Rather, the train wears numerous hats.

When inaugurated in February 2000, the *Royal Canadian Pacific* was essentially a string of elegant, historic, and underemployed CPR business cars, all built in the 1920s by the railroad's own Angus Shops

in Montreal, plus a sleeper crafted from a parlor car of like provenance. Meals were served in the dining rooms of some of the business cars—until 2003, when a diner and second sleeper, also constructed within the shells of vintage heavyweight cars, were added to the consist. This boosted capacity from 23 to 32, helping profitability. Though the train is active virtually all year, some 70 percent of its trips are charters; only a half dozen or so excursions a year are offered to the public. With tours off the train, fine cuisine, and a warmly woody ambiance, the *RCP* is a slightly more exquisite (and decidedly more intimate) version of the *GrandLuxe Express*.

In addition, the cars are used by CPR as they always had been, for corporate travel and for entertaining good customers. Part of the *Royal Canadian Pacific* project was the stylish glass-enclosed Pavillion, connected to Calgary's Palliser Hotel (built in 1914 by CPR) and very rentable for events. It includes a train shed that is the *RCP*'s home when not on the road. Yet another part of the project has been the restoration of Hudson No. 2816, which sometimes powers the handsome, historic train, decked out in traditional maroon. The Canadian Pacific Railway, the nation's first transcontinental line, is an icon for Canadians. Current management is proud of this heritage and sees the train as an excellent public-relations tool.

Though a long-running success, the Tucson-based (though operating in Mexico) *Sierra Madre Express*, which carries tourists to the Copper Canyon, is a horse of a very different color. With equipment that is fun, funky, and historic rather than luxurious, it runs on a relative shoestring. Its roots go back to one of the cars still in the consist, *Chile Verde*. Peter Robbins, *SME*'s owner, bought it—a 16-duplex-roomette, 4–double bedroom sleeper built for Great Northern's *Empire Builder*—for $3,500 back in the 1970s as a place to live while working as a mining consultant at the Massachusetts Institute of Technology. When

An F-unit in heritage Canadian Pacific Railway dress heads the *Royal Canadian Pacific* on a misty morning in Banff. *Karl Zimmermann.*

BELOW: Conviviality aboard the *Mount Stephen*, a business car built in 1926 in CPR's Angus Shops. It now serves as the tail car on the *Royal Canadian Pacific*. *Karl Zimmermann.*

Robbins moved to Tucson, the car (by then much modified to serve as a residence) went along too; with the *Arizona,* a round-end observation built in 1948 for Northern Pacific's *North Coast Limited,* in 1981 it became the first *Sierra Madre Express.*

The train grew modestly over the next quarter century, until by 2006 it included six cars, the most notable a dome diner built for Union Pacific's *City of Portland.* Arizona Rail Car, Robbins's sister enterprise, which does contract repair work on freight and passenger cars, dovetails nicely with the *SME* and moderates maintenance costs (a benefit that Colorado Railcar will no doubt bring to GrandLuxe Rail). The *Sierra Madre Express* typically operates about six tours a year on its own, and in addition the train is chartered to Tauck Tours for some 20 trips a year—another significant and reliable boost to *SME*'s bottom line.

Another private tour train that has grown incrementally and now thrives is the *Rocky Mountaineer.* Created by VIA Rail Canada in 1988 and initially called *Canadian Rockies by Daylight* (a name that perhaps inspired "Montana Daylight," a similar service that would ultimately fall into the failure category), this ten-car train, intended for sightseeing rather than transportation, ran between Vancouver and Jasper or Calgary (with an all-important stop at nearby Banff); passengers were off-loaded at Kamloops, British Columbia, the journey's approximate midpoint. Equipment was "Daynighter" chair cars, somewhat spiffed up—conversions of conventional coaches made decades earlier by Canadian National. Generous seat spacing and the addition of leg rests enhanced their attractiveness for overnight travel but actually compromised their utility as sightseeing vehicles, since seat-to-window alignments were skewed.

In late 1989, VIA hit a buzz-saw of budget cutting, which would force the company to eliminate more than half its service in early 1990. Looking for pieces of the network that might attract a buyer, they found only the tourist train by then called the "Rocky Mountaineer." Peter R. B. Armstrong, who

had been an executive vice-president for Gray Line but was then looking for something to do, thought it could be a big success and led a team to acquire it, becoming president and CEO of Great Canadian Railtour Company, the train's owner.

And it has been a big success, though not before some perilous years early on. A major reason for this eventual prosperity has been the splendid Ultra Domes delivered by Tom Rader, now numbering 16, that *Rocky Mountaineer* operates as its premium "Gold Leaf" option. Another secret to success surely has been the daytime-only nature of the service, which satisfies the scenery-hungry tourist while eliminating the substantial expense of operating sleeping cars. (Armstrong had requested a tour of the *American Orient Express* in February 1996 when the train was in winter lay-up in Denver, and on that occasion he and Greg Mueller traded ideas on the pros and cons of daytime versus sleeper excursions.) The daytime-running-only scenario has attracted imitators, including the *Montana Daylight* and VIA's Jasper-Prince Rupert *Skeena,* which unloads passengers for the night in Prince George—and happens to include in its consist a Rader Railcar single-level dome intended for the *Florida Fun Train.*

Beginning in 2006, the company added a third route, over Canadian National's former BC Rail line. The *Whistler Mountaineer* operates between North Vancouver and the resort town of Whistler, with first-class passengers accommodated in single-level dome cars. A traditional *Rocky Mountaineer* consist operates between Whistler and Jasper, with an overnight layover in Quesnel.

That's the short list of successes; the tally of failures is much longer and includes *Montana Daylight* and the *Whistler Northlander,* the forerunner of the *Whistler Mountaineer,* which went down in 2002 with all BC Rail passenger service when provincial funding was withdrawn. It includes the *Florida Fun Train,* the enterprise whose fate became entangled with that of Rader Railcar, and the San Francisco-Los Angeles "California Sun Express," a brief attempt in 1990 by Princess Cruises to find employment for

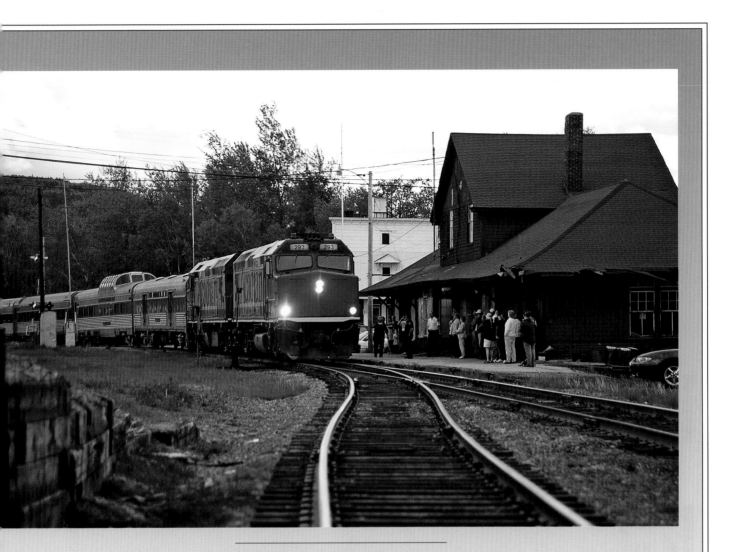

The *Acadian* pulls in to Jackman, Maine, on June 9, 2002. *Roger Cook.*

three of the ex–Milwaukee Road Tour Alaska domes created by Tom Rader and made obsolete in Alaska by his revolutionary Ultra Domes.

The "California Sun Express" was hauled by Amtrak's *Coast Starlight,* a tag-along approach that Amtrak tried on its own behalf with the "Keystone Classic Club," run as an adjunct to its New York City-Pittsburgh *Pennsylvanian.* Inaugurated on August 1, 1991, this twice-a-week service was operated with a single private car, the *J. Pinckney Henderson,* which had begun life as a 72-seat coach built in 1954 for the Missouri-Kansas-Texas (Katy) by Pullman-Standard (as its first all-stainless-steel car). "Keystone Classic Club" was the pet project of Paul M. Weyrich, founder of the ultra-conservative Heritage

Foundation and, at the time, a member of the Amtrak board. The *J. Pinckney* had been purchased as a derelict hulk by North Carolinian Robert Willetts and converted for charter with rear-facing windows, lounge chairs, dining tables, and private bedrooms that could be converted for day use to private dining room and library. In spite of elegant surroundings and fine meals served with a flourish, the "Keystone Classic Club" survived for less than a year—a victim of the eternally changing landscape at Amtrak and, perhaps, the lack of touristic cachet with Pittsburgh as a destination.

A casualty of roughly the same period was Transcisco Tours *Sierra 49er Express,* a San Francisco Bay Area-to-Reno train with far more populist aspira-

Pennsylvania's Horseshoe Curve as seen through the windows of the *J. Pinckney Henderson,* in service as Amtrak's *Keystone Classic Club. Karl Zimmermann.*

tions, which was inaugurated on December 7, 1990. Tricked out in eye-catching (some might have said garish) maroon and baby blue, the train offered two classes of service: standard, in rebuilt ex–Southern-Pacific/Caltrain bilevel commute cars, and luxury dome, using ex–Union Pacific dome lounges converted for meal service by Scenic Rail Dining, their previous owner. Amtrak had run its *Reno Fun Train* on this route, but the *Sierra 49er Express* promised to be even more fun—and funkier, with, eventually, a dance car with cabaret tables, a piano lounge, handwriting analysts, and magicians. But the train proved to have no more magic than the *Florida Fun Train,* somewhat similar in concept. The *Sierra 49er Express* made its last run on April 29, 1991, and the costs of construction and operation led Transcisco Industries, the parent company, to file for Chapter 11 protection.

And then, most recently, there's the regrettable failure of The Acadian Railway Company, the final in a series of never-fully-successful ventures by Randy Parten's Denver Railway Car Company. Houston-based though subsequently operating in diverse areas of North America, Parten first ran the *Texas*

Limited excursion from that city, using a number of the cars that became staples of his later trains as well: an ex–New York Central round-end observation, ex–*California Zephyr* dome coach *Silver Stirrup,* and dome diner *Maroon Bells,* originally a Missouri Pacific dome coach. This diner was named for a mountain in the Aspen, Colorado, area, reflecting Parten's aspiration to establish passenger service between Denver and Aspen as the Roaring Fork Railroad. With success seemingly in sight, the project finally fell to the "not-in-my-backyard" forces in upscale Aspen.

The cars from the *Texas Limited*—along with a second *CZ* dome coach, *Silver Colt*—served for a number of years beginning in 1993 on the *South Orient Express,* Parten's excursion between Chihuahua City and Los Mochis that served the Copper Canyon. A competitor of the *Sierra Madre Express* (though exclusively a daylight train, with all overnights in hotels), the *SOE* never became firmly established. Then came *The Acadian,* a tour train that brought Parten's spiffy Budd-built train to New England and into eastern Canada. Its main route was between Montreal and Saint John, New Brunswick, via the Moosehead Lake region in Maine or, seasonally, Montreal and Portland, Maine. In addition, the company placed one or more of its luxury cars on Amtrak's Montreal-New York City *Adirondack;* called the *Lake Champlain,* this connecting service was designed to link the major northeastern population centers with Montreal.

Unfortunately, *The Acadian*'s launch occurred in 2002, in the severely depressed travel market in the wake of September 11. The train limped through the season with modest load factors. Though a brochure for 2003 was prepared and distributed, not a single departure actually occurred that year, and Randy Parten's handsome train was dismembered and sold, writing *finis* to a story of multiple chapters.

Back they came to Colorado Railcar for a new coat of paint and a bright new beginning. Three single-level domes intended for the *Florida Fun Train* but never finished ultimately were completed in 2000 for BC Rail's *Whistler Northwind*. When BC Rail shut all its passenger operations in 2002, the cars went to VIA Rail Canada, where they provide "Totem Class" service on the Jasper-Prince Rupert *Skeena*. In the decade after its renaming, Colorado Railcar was busier than ever, building 32 Ultra Domes as compared to the 12 built by Rader Railcar and developing, producing, and marketing a spiffy dome-like DMU—a self-propelled "diesel multiple unit" designed especially for commuter service.

While the *Rocky Mountaineer* would prove to be a Canadian alliance both long-running and highly satisfactory to both parties, a much less auspicious (and essentially unfulfilled) one began much earlier, in 1989, between Rader and Canadian travel promoter Sam Blythe. Blythe had a vision: "The Royal Canadian," an all-new, bi-level, ultra-luxurious cruise train that would roam across Canada. Blythe not only had a vision (which in truth was far more Rader's than his), he had a plan, for a train featuring "Sky Domes," Ultra Dome variants. There would be a dome diner; sleepers with some rooms the full width of the car, completely under glass, with media center and wet bar; and a glass-enclosed end-of-train lounge, with open observation platform on the lower level.

Sam Blythe had brochures and tariffs—even reservations—for this paragon. What the Toronto-based Blythe & Company didn't ever have was a train, which for lack of funds died before a single car was built. Many of the ideas generated by this project later became part of the *Marlboro Unlimited* concept, and, after that ended, the *Golden Eagle*—another promising project that never reached fruition. But down the road lay the *GrandLuxe Express,* which should finally make all these years of planning, and all the false starts, worthwhile.

In 1997, with Thomas Downs as chairman, in yet another attempt to improve its bottom line, Amtrak created a hugely ambitious business plan that had the company moving aggressively into the mail and express business, and in that connection projected (and, in a few cases, actually operated) many additional services. It was this initiative that gave rise to the "Golden Eagle" project. Ed Ellis became head of Amtrak's mail and express division, and a much more modest version of the original plan went forward.

"I'd talked to Amtrak many times about doing something with them," Rader said, "and when they projected a 72-hour train between New York City and Los Angeles to expedite mail and express, they said we could put some luxury passenger cars on it." The plan was for the train to run essentially non-stop but for crew changes, servicing, and passenger stops at Chicago and Lamy, New Mexico. Rader would pay Amtrak a mileage rate to pull his luxury cars. Promotional material was assembled, and Colorado Railcar was poised to begin production of the cars, when a change of management and change of heart at Amtrak scuttled the project. Once again, Rader's dream of a bi-level domed super-train was stymied.

Though they'll have to be largely disassembled and heavily rebuilt because of changes in the Federal Railroad Administration's safety standards promulgated in 1999, the two sleepers and mezzanine lounge car, which were partially built for *Marlboro Unlimited* and then redecorated from a knotty-pine, western ambiance to something more sophisticated as mock-ups for promoting the *Golden Eagle,* will finally roll, assuming present plans hold. So too will a single-level car with an open platform, rebuilt with two bedrooms, living room, dining room, and small kitchen to serve as a private car. When they become reality for the *GrandLuxe Express,* probably joining the consist in the 2009 season, the cars will be a spectacular innovation.

Accommodations aboard the bi-level sleepers will range from the splendid on the lower level (essentially the Grand Suites as they now appear in the Colorado Railcar rebuilds for *AOE* of 2002, *Bar Harbor, Charleston, Denver,* and *Savannah*) to the breathtaking on the upper level, which will contain another six Grand Suites plus a President's Suite and a Chairman's Suite—all under dome glass. (Nighttime privacy will be provided by tambour-styled shades that can be pulled down if desired, but the option of sleeping under the stars no doubt will appeal to many travelers.) The Chairman's Suite, as the name suggests, will be slightly more spacious than the President's Suite. Perhaps the greatest feature of both is the fact that they encompass the full width of the car, with dome glass on both sides, made possible by their location at the ends of the car and the fact that the pass-through between cars is on the lower level.

These cars are perhaps the most exciting changes that Tom Rader had in mind for his new-old train when he acquired it, but far from the only ones.

"What we're trying to do is match our customers' expectations with reality and upgrade the whole product," Rader said shortly after taking over. To accomplish this, GrandLuxe's first priority will be to expand the size of the train, which in fact *AOE* had done with its second train, and then by collapsing the two back into one train, with more sleepers than originally.

"The reality is that the train loses money carrying one hundred passengers," Rader said. "However, we are committed to expanding the public facilities as we expand the number of sleepers. And we want one dining seat per passenger," an enviable situation that *AOE* with the longer trains of its last years couldn't accomplish. "We will also add the second lounge car to the consist as we expand."

Another initiative that was begun immediately, along with a general upgrade of maintenance, was rebuilding the older sleepers by combining Vintage Pullmans, the traditional double bedrooms with uppers and lowers and no showers, into Classic Presidential Suites. The first cars to receive this work, before the 2007 season, were *Monte Carlo* and *Portland.*

"We don't think our customers really want to shower down the hall," Rader explained. "By the end of 2008 we plan to be an all-suite train, with a few singles with showers mixed in. We know that, by combining the smaller rooms, we're cutting revenue potential, but we believe the net result will be higher customer satisfaction and more sales." Grand-Luxe plans to increase to 50 the roughly 35 operating weeks a year that the train has averaged historically, which also will boost revenues. "However," Rader said, "it will take two trainsets to get the business to pay the cost of capital."

The purchase of *AOE* brought with it 30 operable cars. The ideal projected consist, based on parking logistics for the planned itineraries and the power capabilities of three Amtrak "Genesis" units, is a "mirror-image" train of 22 cars: crew cars, four sleepers, lounge car, dome car, diner, three sleepers, diner, dome car, lounge, four sleepers, *New York* observation. That would leave eight cars to rotate in and out of the consist for maintenance, which will allow for an essentially year-round operating season.

"We plan on a total revamping of dining," Rader said. "We've found that people like to dine in the dome, and that's what we'll provide." In one and probably both of the domes, plans call for the downstairs area to be converted to kitchen space. Related to that will be a major itinerary change, with the goal of having the train under way for dinner every night, since changing views are an important component of the dining-car experience.

"The other part of the plan," Rader said, "is, when we can get railroad cooperation, to be moving for breakfast." This of course is more problematic. *AOE*'s itineraries had evolved to call for arrivals in the wee hours, to provide padding so lateness would not disrupt the next day's tours. Running at breakfast hour would eliminate this padding. These tours themselves marked another new direction for GrandLuxe, which now offers passengers a choice of different included tours at some destinations.

The new name, *GrandLuxe Express,* is a significant innovation in itself, and the change was not voluntary, though it's certainly been embraced positively by new management. In fact, *AOE* had lost a legal battle of several years' duration with James Sherwood's Orient-Express Hotels, parent company of the *Venice Simplon-Orient-Express,* over the use of the name "Orient Express." In the 1980s, apparently, Sherwood had gone to the French government to license that name, the rights to which were held by SNCF (La Société Nationale des Chemins de Fer, France's national railway). *AOE* argued its case, ultimately unsuccessfully. Having lost a suit in Canada, they decided to settle in the United States. They were able to postpone the change, though a final deadline of December 31, 2006, was set for the name to be removed from the cars and elsewhere. This was done after the train had completed its trans-Canada trips in October and returned to Fort Lupton, via a repositioning trip from Seattle for travel agents and "Golden Railers," as *AOE* called and GLR now calls past passengers.

"The challenge," as Rader explained, "had been to find a name that could be registered—and that accurately described the product." Since *AOE* had known for some time that it would be forced to rebrand, the company had retained Landor Associates, a branding and design consultancy with a worldwide reputation and client base. Landor came up with, in Rader's words, "some very exotic names," but none that seemed right to him (and, as the sale moved toward formal completion, it became his prerogative to choose). He wasn't sorry to lose the "Orient Express" name.

"'American Orient Express' only has meaning for those who have traveled on the train," Rader said, "and they're unhappy with the change. To the balance of the world, the name is meaningless. Furthermore, we want to operate in Canada and Mexico, so the train shouldn't be called 'American.'" In fact, *AOE* salespeople had always reported that the first question they had to answer inevitably concerned their train's relation or lack thereof to its (distant) European cousin. Management actually had been casting about for new names as far back as 1995, when Mueller had suggested "American Overland Expeditions," though as long as the Swiss had been involved the old name was apparently secure, through their *Nostalgie Istanbul Orient Express.*

Though the GrandLuxe purchase, and the prospect of bi-level cars and eventually a complete bi-level train, may have seemed a bolt from the blue to outside observers, bi-level musings by *AOE* actually go back a decade. In fact, in September 1995 T. C. Swartz and Greg Mueller visited the Rader Railcar facility and met with Tom Rader and Tom Janaky (who was then vice-president of sales and marketing, which he would be for Rader and then Colorado Railcar for 16 years before moving over to GrandLuxe) to explore the possibilities of *AOE*'s expansion with Rader equipment. By June of 1997 Mueller was talking with Amtrak officials about the equipment, motive power, and logistical challenges that would ensue from a 1999 launch of a bi-level trainset, and that same year he introduced Rader and Henry Hillman. The expansion of *AOE* with Rader bi-level equipment never came to pass, though Hillman of course did order four single-level sleepers from Rader.

On May 31, almost immediately after the purchase by GrandLuxe, the consolidation of *AOE*'s disparate operations began. Those in Downers Grove, Denver, Portland, and Tenino were moved to Evergreen, Colorado, in the Denver area, near Colorado Railcar's facility in Fort Lupton, and to that facility itself. The process concluded ahead of schedule in late August, with the Tenino facility the last to close. This consolidation meant an almost entirely new staff.

The GrandLuxe itineraries also looked quite different from *AOE*'s. For one thing, there were only four: "GrandLuxe Mexico" (which, as it turned out, would at first be greatly altered and frequencies curtailed before finally being canceled altogether), "National Parks of the West," "The Great Northwest & Rockies," and "Rockies, Sierras & Napa." Gone from the previous (*AOE*) year were the "Pacific Coast Explorer" (doomed in part by inadequate siding lengths, at Paso Robles particularly, for an expanded consist), "Antebellum South" (which, after being cut back in the wake of Katrina from New Orleans to Savannah, was much diminished), the "American Southwest," the "Great Transcontinental Rail Journey," and the "Grand Trans-Canada Rail Journey."

The objective for the first GrandLuxe season, according to Rader, was to perfect a few itineraries, build confidence in the product, and attract new riders by offering those trips that had proven most popular in the past. For 2008, other trips would be added.

"We are in negotiation with Canadian National," Rader said. "In 2008 we expect to do some Canadian transcontinental trips, and some

Canadian Rockies circle trips as well." Also projected for the future is operation in Alaska.

Some of the bad luck that seemed to dog the *American Orient Express* in Mexico hit GrandLuxe when it wasn't yet four months old, and then shortly thereafter dealt it a second blow. In a reversal, Ferrocarril Mexicano declined to operate the *GrandLuxe Express* on its line south from Sufragio to Mazatlán, Guadalajara, and Mexico City. "After four and a half months of negotiating a contract with Ferromex," Rader told a group of Golden Railers visiting his Fort Lupton facility after the positioning journey from Seattle, "two days before signing, they reneged. They decided they were too busy to handle us." With an ambitious program of 26 departures advertised, extending from the end of October through April, this was a blow. "With all the promotion we'd done for this program, and the bookings we'd already received, this created a loss for us of $2½ to 3 million," Rader said.

GLR's first response was to delay the start of the Mexico season until late January, and substitute a shorter itinerary—over better maintained Kansas City Southern de Mexico tracks—for the one originally planned. Seven nights long overall, with just three on the train, between Monterrey and Mexico, the tour's U.S. base would have been San Antonio, with air connection between there and Monterrey. Then, after more money had been spent promoting it, this itinerary was also canceled. The primary reasons: simply not enough lead time to publicize and book it, and the too lengthy process for KCSM to get a needed passenger transportation certificate.

In May of 2007, some intriguing innovations were revealed by GLR, mostly for the 2008 season. A limited number of premium accommodations, called Gold Suites, will be available in the *Portland* sleeper. These rooms will feature side-by-side lower berths. Also new will be the Triple Suites: adjoining Parlor Suites and Single Sleepers with a door between, sleeping three.

New and updated itineraries abound. "Grand Canyon and the Southwest," from Scottsdale to Santa Fe, and "Western and Pacific Coast Treasures," from Santa Fe to Seattle, are new (though the latter in effect combines part of the national parks itinerary with the old "Pacific Coast Explorer." "National Parks of the West" will be tweaked, as will "Rockies, Sierras & Napa." "Great Northwest and Rockies" changes its name to "Great Northwestern National Parks."

Most interesting is the inauguration of the "GrandLuxe Limited" program, which begins in November 2007 and extends into January 2008. It calls for the train's being split in three, each section with sleepers, diner, and lounge car. One consist will operate between Washington, D.C., and Miami as a part of Amtrak's *Silver Meteor*, one between Chicago and Los Angeles as part of the *Southwest Chief*, and one between Chicago and San Francisco as part of the *California Zephyr*. Just two or three days long, these trips can introduce the train to travelers who may not be willing to commit to one of the longer trips and will appeal to those attracted more to the rail travel itself than to the off-train tours.

Also worth noting: This in effect brings the train full circle, back to the concept of piggybacking on Amtrak's trains, as the *American-European Express* initially did.

First Henry Hillman and now Tom Rader have realized that increased passenger volume—accomplished through both more departures and a longer train—is essential for profitability. With 21 cars, requiring three Amtrak Genesis diesels as power, the 2007 train is the longest ever: *Los Angeles, Yellowstone Park, Grand Canyon, Monterey, Vienna, Monte Carlo, Bar Harbor, Santa Fe, Charleston, Rocky Mountain, Chicago, Zurich, Copper Canyon, Seattle, Portland, Washington, Denver, Paris, Montreal, Savannah,* and *New York.*

Though the inclusion of a second flat-top lounge in the consist (the *Rocky Mountain,* now a "library lounge," with the piano removed) helps mitigate overcrowding, this unprecedentedly long consist does inevitably have drawbacks. The round-end observation *New York* is a favorite of many passengers, but those berthed in the first sleeper, for instance, face a trek through 15 cars to reach it. In addition, train length also often forces uninspiring industrial locations for boarding and detraining, since 21 cars aren't easily accommodated.

Though GrandLuxe is off to a rocky start, Tom Rader is optimistic. "I always wanted to be back in the tour business," he had said shortly after the sale, "and I thought that, in general, what *AOE* was doing was close to the model I wanted to follow." Now he has the chance to realize some long-held dreams—of creating perhaps the most luxurious passenger train ever.

Colorado Railcar Manufacturing's "mezzanine car," a design first conceived for the never-completed *Marlboro Unlimited,* has a bar-lounge and viewing gallery above and baby grand and dance floor below. *Colorado Railcar.*

This view through the dome window shows the room layout and amenities for an upper-level Grand Suite aboard the bi-level sleepers that are in the *GrandLuxe Express*'s probable future. *Colorado Railcar.*

The Chairman's Suite is the most spacious and glamorous of the bi-level sleepers' rooms, with views to both sides of the train. *Colorado Railcar.*

The newest Ultra Dome design is for the *Wilderness Express* cars, 18 feet tall, built for Royal Caribbean and Celebrity Cruise Line's joint service in Alaska. *Colorado Railcar.*

Tom Rader at the Colorado Railcar facility in Fort Lupton. *Karl Zimmermann.*

The *Rocky Mountaineer* operates 16 Ultra Domes in its elegant "Gold Leaf" service. Dining is on the lower level, sightseeing above. *Karl Zimmermann.*

Though the *GrandLuxe Express* began the 2007 season with blank letterboards, the words "American Orient Express" expunged as required by legal agreement, Photoshop artistry predicts how the train will appear in the future. *GrandLuxe Rail Journeys.*

Innovations marking the *GrandLuxe Express*'s first full season in 2007: the diner fully set with GrandLuxe china, and lounge car *Rocky Mountain* without a piano. *Karl Zimmermann.*

Sleeper *Santa Fe,* formerly Union Pacific's *Star Crest,* gleams in the evening light in Jasper. *Karl Zimmermann.*

5

Silk Purses

GrandLuxe's Glamorous Cars

Of the 31 cars included in GrandLuxe's purchase of the *American Orient Express,* 11 had been owned by *American-European Express,* and another 3 had been used by *AEE* under lease from John Kirkwood's Rail Ventures. Of those 11 with *AEE* heritage, 5 remain among GrandLuxe's signature cars, and the others are in service as well. Among the most memorable are the two virtually identical mid-train lounge cars, originally called "club cars" and later "piano lounges," named *Bay Point Club* and *St. Moritz* in *AEE* service and rechristened *Seattle* and *Rocky Mountain* in 1996 by *AOE.* These have been the only *AEE* cars to receive new names.

The *AOE* (and now GrandLuxe) car names virtually all offer interesting clues to the train's history. "Bay Point Club," the name of Bill Spann's Panama City enterprise, obviously became meaningless when his involvement with the train ended. TCS Expeditions is Seattle-based, so the change from *Bay Point Club* to *Seattle* was logical. Though *AOE* retained all the other European car names assigned by *AEE—Berlin, Istanbul, Monte Carlo, Paris, Vienna, Zurich*—the temptation to rechristen *St. Moritz* (with its lovely, lighted murals of snowcapped mountains) *Rocky Mountain,* an important itinerary element for the new *AOE,* must have been irresistible.

These two elegant cars began life as Union Pacific 14-section sleepers, *Alpine Meadow* and *Alpine View,* delivered by American Car & Foundry in 1954. Already dinosaurs when built, since uppers and lowers in open sections had fallen out of fashion by then, these sleepers were converted in 1965 to 44-seat coaches, which were sold to Amtrak in 1973. It would take a mystic to stand in one of the cars today and divine its humble heritage, so brilliant is the transformation wrought by Bill and Melissa Spann.

As configured for *AEE,* tucked behind the restrooms were compact two-berth crew cabins, space that would no longer be needed for that purpose once *AOE* added cars exclusively dedicated to housing (and feeding) crew. Beginning the week after Christmas in 1995 and continuing through the following March, considerable reconfiguration of equipment was done at TransTexas Rail's facilities in San Antonio to ready the train for its first season under the sole management of TCS Expeditions. The TransTexas Rail operation had two sides: train charter, with George Pierce in charge, and the car and locomotive shop, directed by Harold Schroeder. The shop, located in a former Southern Pacific facility east of San Antonio, did contract work on freight and passenger cars and diesels.

Aboard both piano lounges, bulkhead murals were replaced by bookshelves for an on-board library, stocked especially with rail and regional titles. In the car then being renamed *Seattle,* the crew space was converted to a compact Passenger Service Office, which came to be universally known as the "PSO." Roughly the equivalent of a shipboard purser's office or hotel front desk, it would be open 24 hours a day as the nerve center for all passenger-related matters. Its public face was a small window reminiscent of a depot ticket-office wicket, with a counter and vertical brass bars. The PSO was also the train's communications center, important at a time when cellular phones and satellite global positioning systems were being introduced. The PSO conversion completed the winter's work; in fact, it was finished en route to Los Angeles for the first departure of the 1996 season.

When the two *American-European Express* consists had been joined as the *Greenbrier Limited,* the train acquired yet more lounge space with the addition of the *New York.* The observation end's deep windows and elevation still provide the excellent visibility that led to the area's being dubbed "Lookout Lounge" by the New York Central. A large, rectangular bar fills the car's center, with the *AEE* logo on the back bar, and the rounded observation area features a circular, tufted, high-backed settee. Like the *Rocky Mountain* and *Seattle* lounges, *New York* remained for *AOE* much as *AEE* created it—though there have obviously been numerous changes in the "soft goods" (that is, carpets and upholstery), and some ongoing rearrangement of furniture. (As a generalization, there came to be more furniture, as the passenger capacity of the train was pushed up for revenue enhancement.)

Diners *Chicago* and *Zurich* as well were largely unchanged in the transition, though the separate "executive dining rooms" with round tables for five at the ends of the cars opposite the kitchen were replaced by the traditional square tables for four and two that fill the balance of the diners, which now seat 42 and 46 respectively. Like *Rocky Mountain* and *Seattle,* these cars have been distinctly upwardly mobile. *Zurich* began life as a café-lounge, built by American Car & Foundry in 1949 for service on Union Pacific's *City* trains; later, it was rebuilt by the railroad to lunch counter–diner-lounge configuration. A decade younger, *Chicago,* built in 1959 by St. Louis Car Company, was a mundane counter-diner-lounge right from the start. Union Pacific sold both cars to Alaska Railroad. Then *AEE* bought them and dramatically elevated them in station. Once Spartan, they became (and remain) opulent reminders of Wagons-Lits luxury.

Though the six original sleepers retained the basic décor provided by *AEE,* they were altered in configuration by *AOE* in the 1995–1996 makeover. *Paris* and *Istanbul,* sister cars built in 1950 by Pullman-Standard for Southern Pacific's Oakland-Portland *Cascade,* were originally 4-compartment, 4–double bedroom, 2–drawing room sleepers (and originally anonymous, since SP didn't name its lightweight sleepers, though most railroads did). For *AEE* they were configured largely as built, with the space marketed under their (essentially) original names: "Private Compartment," "Private Bedroom," or "Drawing Room," with a "Master Suite" combination available by combining drawing rooms and compartments with a connecting doorway. An office for the *chef de train* replaced one compartment.

AOE, however, paired two sets of bedrooms and compartments into "Presidential Suites," ten of which were created by the 1995–1996 conversions, a dramatic addition to the sparse two offered by *AEE*'s consist when combined for the *Greenbrier Limited.* This left intact the two drawing rooms as well as three or four of the compartments and bedrooms (including, aboard *Paris,* the one that had been an office), which eventually *AOE* and then GrandLuxe lumped together as "Vintage Pullman" rooms, a more honest description than the "Deluxe Sleeper" or "Superior Sleeper" that *AOE* had called them for a time. Drawing rooms were renamed "Parlor Suites" by *AOE,* a designation they retain. Since the double-size Presidential Suites, which would remain the premier accommodation for a decade, were created from what were essentially traditional bedroom suites, the redundant second toilet annexes were converted to private showers. All cars also had a public shower for passengers in Parlor Suite and Vintage Pullman accommodations—and Single Sleepers, essentially Vintage Pullmans sold for individual occupancy. (Much later, for the 2004 season, showers would be installed in the toilet annexes of the Parlor Suites, with those spaces doing double duty, as they do in Amtrak's current bedrooms.

As built, *Vienna* and *Berlin* were sister cars with 11 bedrooms each, delivered in 1956 by Pullman-Standard to Union Pacific for *City* train service as *Placid Waters* and *Placid Lake. AEE* turned a pair of bedrooms aboard each car into a "Presidential Cabin" (as that company called them), and *AOE* did the same thing with another pair, yielding two Presidential Suites and eight Vintage Pullmans per car.

American Orient Express began the practice of naming Parlor and Presidential Suites. The train's four Parlor Suites honored Collis P. Huntington, Leland Stanford, Charles Crocker, and Mark Hopkins—the Central Pacific's "Big Four" quartet of financiers. All the Presidential Suites were named for United States presidents, though one of *Vienna*'s was later renamed "Henry L. Hillman." U.S. presidents honored were John Quincy Adams, Grover Cleveland, Dwight D. Eisenhower, William Henry Harrison, Andrew Jackson, Thomas Jefferson, Lyndon B. Johnson, John F. Kennedy, Abraham Lincoln, William McKinley, Franklin Delano Roosevelt, Theodore Roosevelt, William Howard Taft, Harry S. Truman, Martin Van Buren, George Washington, and Woodrow Wilson—and Ulysses S. Grant, who was deleted from *Vienna* to make way for Hillman.

Washington and *Monte Carlo* were both Pullman-Standard 10-roomette, 6–double bedroom sleepers, part of a 75-car order for 10/6's placed by Chesapeake & Ohio in 1946. *Washington* was delivered in 1950 as the *City of Staunton,* which C&O used on the *George Washington, Sportsman, Pere Marquette,* and *Resorter.* Identical sister *Monte Carlo* was among 19 cars that never made it to C&O service; when the railroad got cold feet about its postwar passenger enthusiasm, the car went instead to the Baltimore & Ohio for *Capitol Limited* service as its *Opequon.*

This story, no doubt the oddest to emerge from the massive re-equipping of passenger rail fleets across the country following World War II, had C&O's eccentric, aggressive chairman, Robert R. Young, at its center. Wanting his railroad to be an industry leader, Young ordered an astonishing 351 passenger cars from 1944 to 1946 to completely modernize C&O passenger operations—which, truth to tell, were not that extensive to begin with. Because of the flood of car orders received by all of the major builders, delivery was slow, and things changed at C&O in the meantime. Passenger business was off, and finances in general not so good, so at the eleventh hour the railroad cancelled all the orders it could, and scrubbed entirely the *Chessie,* the new flagship it had planned to launch. Other cars that were delivered were immediately resold.

AEE had converted both *Washington* and *Monte Carlo* to 8–Private Bedroom sleepers, with two crew compartments in each. *AOE* in its rebuildings preparatory to the 1996 season made Presidential Suites out of these two crew quads, which had become redundant since the train at the same time was adding crew sleepers. These crew cars were acquired from Amtrak as part of a five-car commitment and named *Grand Canyon*—P-S-built ex-UP 10/6 *Placid Lake* (a sister to *Berlin* and *Vienna* and delivered the same year, 1956)—and *Pacific Star*. Also built in 1956 by Pullman-Standard, this car had begun life as UP 5–double bedroom buffet lounge *La Grande* before its 1965 rebuilding into 11–double bedroom *Star Range*.

The original six guest sleepers, all plain-vanilla postwar lightweights, had gotten makeovers for *AEE* similar to (if perhaps less spectacular than) the lounges and diners: mahogany walls, faux marble in the toilet annexes, opulent fabrics, art on the walls. In *AOE* service, each cabin was equipped with a telephone that rang in the Passenger Service Office. Other small changes were made over time, such as the drawers installed under seats where possible. An expedient no doubt borrowed from yacht design, this was an ingenious way to provide extra storage space, much needed in accommodations originally designed for one- or two-night stays rather than tours of a week or more.

Three of the 13 cars originally purchased by *American-European Express* were never refurbished and were eventually sold. These were Chesapeake & Ohio 10/6 *City of Grand Rapids* (built by Pullman-Standard in 1950), sister of the car that became *Washington;* Union Pacific 11–double bedroom *Placid Bay* (Pullman-Standard, 1956), sister of the cars that became *Berlin, Vienna,* and (later, for *AOE*) *Grand Canyon;* and Grand Trunk Western buffet-parlor-lounge *Diamond Lake* (Pullman-Standard, 1954).

The consist had grown only by one during the brief TransTexas era when, in December 1994, George Pierce added the *San Antonio*—an ex-army hospital car used by *AOE* as baggage-laundry-shop car. (Once again, the car's name is a clue to the time of its joining the train.) John Kirkwood's three sleepers, which first entered the picture in the *AEE* years, would be leased by *AOE* (and eventually purchased at the Grand-Luxe transition), moving in and out of the consist as needed and eventually becoming regular cars. Kirkwood's *Bella Vista,* an 11–double bedroom sleeper built in 1950 by Pullman-Standard for C&O as *Home-*

stead, was named "Portland" when painted into *AOE* cream, blue, and gold—during the Hillman era, obviously, with the name again being a giveaway. This car had been modestly rebuilt by Kirkwood as a private car, with a small lounge at one end.

Another of Kirkwood's cars, the *Montecito* (built in 1950 by Pullman-Standard as 5–double bedroom café-lounge *City of Cleveland* for the Nickel Plate Road) became *AOE*'s *San Francisco,* serving as a dining car for crew and providing two Presidential Suites and two Vintage Pullmans for passengers. The third Kirkwood car, his *Monterey,* which has kept its name, has an interesting, even illustrious history. Another one of Chesapeake & Ohio's postwar orphans, this 5–double bedroom buffet lounge observation was delivered by Pullman-Standard to the C&O in 1950 as *Wolverine Club,* but the next year it went to the Baltimore & Ohio, beginning a long career as the *Wawasee,* carrying the tailsign of the *Capitol Limited,* the line's premier streamliner.

Though the car served *AOE* primarily as crew sleeper and diner, it did have a few opportunities to relive its past glories in the passenger trade. Like Kirkwood's other cars, it ran regularly after the 1991 *AEE* derailment (discussed in chapter 2). Then, at the beginning of the 1998 season, it was pressed into service briefly as a stand-in for *New York* while that car underwent some undercarriage work at the TransTexas Rail facility.

Other cars were leased early in the *AOE* years to fill particular needs. At the beginning of the 1996 season, while work on *Pacific Star* was being completed, the company used as a fill-in crew sleeper 12-bedroom, 4-roomette *Cimarron River* (built by Pullman-Standard in 1948 for Frisco's *Meteor*), leased from the Marchiando brothers of St. Louis. That same season, needing extra capacity, and interested in experimenting with a dome car, *AOE* added dome lounge *Northern Sky* for some trips. Built by American Car & Foundry for UP in 1955, this *Auto-Train* veteran had been reconfigured by Northern Rail Car in 1992. In 1997, for the same reasons, management leased *Columbia River,* another UP dome, this one a diner, built for the *City of Portland.*

This is the roster of cars that would serve through the TCS Expeditions years and well into Henry Hillman's ownership, right up to the addition of a second train in 2002. Obviously, that expansion opened the floodgates to new cars, many of which have become the core of the train that GrandLuxe Rail Journeys purchased in 2006. It also initiated an ongoing, never fully resolved struggle to find a few missing pieces of the puzzle of putting into service two perfect consists. This led to a handful of leased cars, some not totally satisfactory, flowing in and out of the consist—at the head end and tail end of the train, as it happened.

The most glamorous additions that came with the creation of an *AOE II* were a pair of full-length dome cars that had been built by the Budd Company in 1955 as "Great Domes" for Great Northern's Chicago-Twin Cities-Seattle/Portland *Empire Builder. Mountain View,* which became the *New Orleans* (a city served on both the "Antebellum South" and southern transcontinental itineraries), was a GN car, while *River View,* which became *Copper Canyon* (named for a region that would be the focus of an itinerary then already advertised for the following season), had been owned by the Chicago, Burlington & Quincy. Though the *Empire Builder* was entirely tricked out in GN's fetching Pullman green and Omaha orange, Burlington, which operated the train from Chicago to the Twin Cities, also contributed to the equipment pool.

These domes, the last operated by Amtrak, had been refurbished and converted to head-end power at the company's Beech Grove Shops. Assigned to the "Special Services Unit," the cars were used in 2000 on the *San Diegan,* the *Reno Fun Train,* and football specials. In early 2001 they went to Beech Grove for truck replacement, but budget cuts interfered, and they were sold to *AOE* later in the year. At *AOE*'s shops in Tenino, the cars were given elegant (and identical) interior finishes. Under glass were six tables for four—ideal for dining (except for the long carry from the kitchen of the adjacent diner), a service into which they soon would be pressed, especially after the two trains were reconsolidated into one and the additional sleepers in the consist necessitated more dining space. In addition, at the ends of the car were inward-facing curved banquettes (with narrow tables in front), seating 40. This upper level became the venue for on-board lectures, replacing the piano lounges, which hadn't served this function nearly as well. In addition to providing more seating, the dome offers passengers the chance to enjoy the scenery while listening.

Downstairs was a bar, a spacious Passenger Service Office, and a small but attractive lounge area. *New Orleans* was the first to enter service, in April of 2002, some months before the second train began. It replaced piano lounge *Seattle,* which later would be deployed as part of *AOE II,* along with dome *Copper Canyon.*

A no less important addition coming with the second train were four essentially all-new sleepers—*Denver, Savannah, Bar Harbor,* and *Charleston*—created within the shells of 44-seat chair cars built for Union Pacific by St. Louis Car Company. (*Bar Harbor* has a 1964 skin, the others 1960; these UP coaches were among the last cars built prior to Amtrak for long-haul service.) The cars were converted at Colorado Railcar, providing the first apparent contact of two companies whose fates would become tightly linked a few years later. The cars would contain seven excellently designed doubles, at first called "Deluxe Suites" and priced just under Presidential Suites. (Initial reaction to the rooms was so positive that the following season they were named "Grand Suites" and became the train's premier accommodations.) There was also one single room—tiny, and a rough rider for being pushed at the far end of the car, over the wheels, but given an attractive private shower in compensation.

The layout of these sleepers had some history, since it was essentially the lower-level floor plan of the cars that would have served on *Marlboro Unlimited* or the *Golden Eagle*. (The only difference was the addition of the single room in space taken up on the bi-levels by a steward's closet and the stairs to the upper level.) With its sofa, table, and facing window-side chair, the daytime configuration of the suites is reminiscent of Amtrak's current "Bedroom," but the similarity ends there. Richly paneled in dark wood, with lush upholstery, handy storage in cabinets above the sofa and in a spacious closet (more spacious than any other closets aboard at any rate), and well-arranged shower and toilet annexes and in-room basins, these suites are worthy of their preeminence. At night, the sofa makes into a bed perpendicular to the window and the chair and table into another one parallel to the window.

Like dome *New Orleans,* sleepers *Savannah* and *Denver* entered service in the spring of 2002; *Bar Harbor* and *Charleston* followed in the fall, when the second train was launched. The name "Bar Harbor" proved a perhaps anomalous choice, since by 2003, the car's first full year in service, the problematic "Autumn in New England & Quebec" itinerary had been revamped and no longer included Bar Harbor, which never actually had been reached by the train itself but only by bus tour from Bangor.

Two other new sleepers, *Santa Fe* and *Montreal,* both refurbished at *AOE*'s own shops in Tenino into cars with three Presidential Suites and five Vintage Pullmans each, rounded out the pool. These ex–Union Pacific cars are exact sisters to crew sleeper *Pacific Star,* with identical histories: built by Pullman-Standard in 1956 as 5–double bedroom buffet lounges—*Santa Fe* was *Cheyenne, Montreal* was *North Platte*—and rebuilt in 1965 into 11–double bedroom *Star Crest* and *Star Scene.*

That took care of the sleepers, and the new domes covered the need for mid-train lounge space, leaving the daunting task of finding an appropriate running mate for the glamorous observation *New York* and diners as elegant as *Chicago* and *Zurich*. The company came close with the diners, though for all but one of the two-plus years that it operated two consists, an adequately attractive tail car proved elusive. Luckily for *AOE,* funding restraints forced BC Rail to discontinue on October 31, 2002, both its Budd Rail Diesel Car–operated *Cariboo Prospector* and its luxury *Whistler Northwind.* With termination in the offing for BC Rail's trains, *AOE* was able to acquire *Whistler Northwind*'s twin-unit dining car for the start-up of *AOE II.*

The cars had been built by American Car & Foundry in 1953 as a dormitory-kitchen/dining room–waiting lounge pair for Union Pacific's *City of Denver.* They'd served on the *Indiana Dinner Train,* where the diner acquired a handsome frosted-glass window depicting a streamlined diesel locomotive. While working for BC Rail, the dining room had received an attractive if folk-arty, whimsical above-window mural depicting along-the-way scenes in British Columbia. Murals aside, the car had an unabashed and not unpleasant streamliner-era feel, but this made it out of step with the ambiance of wood-paneled luxury that informed all the other cars. And in spite of being furnished entirely with tables seating four (as opposed to the more spacious and gracious four-and-two arrangement in *Zurich* and *Chicago*), its capacity of 60 fell well short of the 88 the original pair could seat. For their new careers, the dining car was dubbed "Jasper" and the kitchen car "Vancouver."

American Orient Express never would field a second observation quite as special as *New York,* though it did in successive seasons couple two interesting cars to *AOE II.* For the first, abbreviated season, the company leased a splendid car, but one that was too different in style and décor to be exactly suitable. That was the Budd-built 3–double bedroom, 1–drawing room buffet-lounge dome observation *Silver Solarium,* once the *California Zephyr*'s feature car, and a glamorous one at that. Built in 1948 for Chicago, Burlington & Quincy, the car carried the *CZ*'s markers from the train's inauguration the following year until its demise in 1970. After more than a decade under the Amtrak banner, it was sold into private charter service. In June 2002 it was acquired by Rail Journeys West, which just months later leased it for use on *AOE II.*

In 2003, the first full season of two-train operation, *AOE* featured another unique second observation, another car owned by *AOE* director John Kirkwood and leased to the company. Called *Glacier Park* in *AOE* service, the car had been built by American Car & Foundry in 1955 as a dome observation-lounge for Union Pacific's *City of Portland.*

It later served on *Auto-Train* as a nightclub car. By the time it reached the *American Orient Express,* it had been dramatically transformed for its role as feature car *Northern View* in Wisconsin & Southern's business train—a handsome assemblage of equipment posh enough that it was chartered by Bill Gates for a tour with family and friends.

At Northern Rail Car (like the Wisconsin & Southern, a William Gardner enterprise), the car's main level was given a classic business-car configuration. The most obvious change was the addition of an open observation platform (which, unfortunately, could only be used in certain supervised circumstances in *AOE* service). The original coach-style seating in the dome was replaced by settees, parlor car–style swivel chairs, banquettes, and tables. The under-dome area was transformed to a dining room, not much use to *AOE,* and a galley was added. The rear portion of the car was a large, wood-paneled (in Honduran mahogany), lushly upholstered lounge with overstuffed furniture. Kirkwood acquired this car, along with sleeper *Gallatin River,* as part of a package when Northern Rail Car filed for Chapter 11 protection.

Prior to its year on the *American Orient Express,* this car (along with *Gallatin River*) had served as the up-market option, dubbed "Montana Gold," for the *Montana Daylight* operation. Presumably, *AOE* might have liked to use *Glacier Park* the following season as well, but Kirkwood opted to sell the car to Patrick Henry's Creative Charters, where it ran as *Warren R. Henry.* Once again the *AOE* quest for a second tail car was on.

The solution, a compromise at best, was to use a car already on hand: a dome lounge, once a Great Northern short-dome chair car that had been a running mate of *Copper Canyon* and *New Orleans* in their "Great Dome" days on the *Empire Builder.* It had been part of the *Montana Daylight* operation since its inception in 1996; ownership passed to the Oregon Rail Holdings when it purchased that operation in 1998.

The car, though nicely furnished as a lounge, was not an observation (though plans, never realized, did call for cutting windows in the hind end) and failed to attract much clientele. Painted red, white, and blue, the car carried the name "American Spirit," the train for which it was intended, on its letterboard above the windows (rather than in the space below them where car names were typically inscribed). Nevertheless, since it had no other name, the car was called "American Spirit" in on-board literature. When the two trains were again collapsed to one after the 2004 season, this dome became surplus. In April 2005 it was sold to Canadian National for use in CN and Illinois Central business-train service.

That took care of the cars for paying passengers, but more crew space was of course needed as well for the second train. In the first season, *Swift Stream*—a 6–double bedroom buffet lounge built in 1949 by Budd for New York Central—served as crew sleeper and diner. (This car, initially acquired for use on *American Spirit*, was sold before GrandLuxe assumed the operation.) The following season, crew sleeper *Colorado River*, leased from St. Louis Car Company's RailCruise America, stood out like a sore (green) thumb toward the front of an otherwise matched consist.

Three additional head-end and crew cars were purchased for the second train and became part of the sale to GrandLuxe. Laundry car *Los Angeles* (a baggage dormitory built by Budd in 1950 for Southern Pacific's *Sunset Limited*), acquired from Illinois Transit, is an alternative to *San Antonio*. Another crew sleeper, Budd-built in 1956 as *Silver Pelican* for Burlington's *Denver Zephyr*, also received an *AOE*-appropriate name: *Yellowstone Park*. It was purchased from the *Michigan Dinner Train*. Already on hand, crew sleeper *Tallahassee* had been part of the five-car commitment from Amtrak made in 1996 that included the sleepers that became *Grand Canyon, Pacific Star, Montreal,* and *Santa Fe. Tallahassee,* an 11–double bedroom car built for Seaboard Air Line by Pullman-Standard in 1956, retains its original configuration—and name, though that Florida Panhandle city has had no connection with the train in any of its incarnations.

When the Hillman interests acquired Montana Rockies Rail Tours in November 1998, many new cars came under Oregon Rail Holdings' umbrella: both those that were already in use on MRRT's *Montana Daylight* and those acquired to outfit the second train projected as part of *American Spirit* service. The lion's share of that equipment was sold to RailQuest America (essentially the original operators of the *Montana Daylight*) when that group of employees and investors bought the company in January 2001. These included three dome cars, a lounge car, a dining car, four coaches, a power car, and a crew car.

Other cars came and went during the Hillman years. The Milwaukee Road "Super Dome" was purchased in August 1998 and sold shortly before the GrandLuxe acquisition. Of the two ex–Union Pacific domes also acquired in August 1998 and once projected for the roles that *Copper Canyon* and *New Orleans* eventually filled, one was sold in June 2005 to Wisconsin & Southern. The other, UP chair car no. 7000, went to GrandLuxe in partially refurbished condition—the thirty-first car included in the sale and the only one that had not operated for *American Orient Express.*

New cars of a very different ilk will no doubt enter the picture following the acquisition by GrandLuxe, though not immediately. Three of the bi-level cars for *Marlboro Unlimited* and later projected for *Golden Eagle* service stood partially completed at Colorado Railcar at the time of the *AOE* purchase. These cars represent the future of the train, and part of the acquisition plan was to complete them and merge them into the otherwise single-level consist, then continue to build bi-levels until there are enough to make up a full trainset. (Car-to-car passage through the bi-levels is on the lower level, making them fully compatible with the conventional cars.) At that point the old cars could be deployed on other routes, possibly in the East.

All this will make 2008 and beyond exciting years of merging the best of the old with the best of the new in equipment and operations.

ABOVE: Sleeper *Washington* is toward the end of the train in this 2001 view of a "Rockies & Yellowstone" run near Plainview, Colorado. *Chip Sherman.*

Chesapeake & Ohio *City of Newport News,* built by Pullman-Standard in 1950, is a sister to *City of Staunton,* now the *Washington.* The stainless-steel fluting on P-S cars (unlike on the Shotwelded cars built by Budd) was merely decorative and has been removed on *Washington. David Randall Collection.*

ABOVE: *AOE*'s elegant diners *Zurich* and *Chicago* started life as Union Pacific counter-diners such as this one. *Union Pacific.*

RIGHT: Elegant marquetry aboard an *AOE* diner. *Steve Patterson.*

BELOW: Breakfast is served aboard *Zurich*. *Karl Zimmermann.*

Union Pacific's *Placid Stream,* shown here on its aisle side, was an 11–double bedroom sleeper built by Pullman-Standard in 1956. *Peter V. Tilp.*

BERLIN
SLEEPING CAR
255

Sister cars to *Placid Stream* are *Placid Waters* (*Vienna,* seen here, also on its aisle side, at Bay Point, Florida), *Placid Lake* (*Berlin*), and *Placid Scene* (crew sleeper *Grand Canyon*). *Bruce C. Nelson.*

INSET: End-door sign. *Joe McMillan.*

ABOVE: Baltimore & Ohio's *Wawasee*, which once proudly carried the tailsign of the *Capitol Limited*, now caters to crew as sleeper/diner *Monterey*. *Peter V. Tilp.*

When crew dine today in this same space aboard the *San Francisco*, they are not served on Pullman's elegant Indian Tree china, as passengers were when the car was Nickel Plate's *City of Cleveland*, as shown here. *Peter V. Tilp Collection.*

Glacier View, built by The Budd Company in 1955 for the *Empire Builder,* was a sister to *Mountain View* and *River View,* currently *GrandLuxe's New Orleans* and *Copper Canyon. Dave Randall Collection.*

RIGHT AND BELOW: *New Orleans,* originally Great Northern's *Mountain View,* was the first of *AOE's* two domes to enter service. *Karl Zimmermann.*

This dome observation, stopped at Grand Junction, Colorado, in August of 1968, is filling its original role as *California Zephyr*'s tail car. *Silver Solarium,* which served *AOE II* in that role in 2002, was one of seven of these splendid cars built for the *CZ. Karl Zimmermann.*

Glacier Park, seen here on the "Autumn in New England & Quebec" train, ran on *AOE II* in 2003. *Jim Shaughnessy.*

A Grand Suite aboard *Denver*, one of the four sleepers rebuilt for *AOE* by Colorado Railcar. *Karl Zimmermann.*

Below: Dining room car *Jasper*, paired with kitchen car *Vancouver*, came to the *American Orient Express* for *AOE II* from BC Rail, which added the murals above the windows for its *Whistler Northwind* service. *Karl Zimmermann.*

Facing page: Inside the observation car *New York. Karl Zimmermann.*

124 ❧

6

Life on Board

"Compact but comfortable." At the pre-boarding briefings at departure hotels that began ten years and more of *American Orient Express* journeys, this caveat had become the alliterative mantra for the tour leaders when they prepared passengers for the initial glimpse of their sleeping quarters. Better that first-time patrons know in advance, for—however clear the brochures may have been about the size of accommodations—sounds of shock, dismay, and rueful laughter inevitably echoed down the corridors of the sleepers after staff had led passengers to their assigned cars and, with the help of their porters, patrons had confronted their rooms. This was, after all, a train.

But no matter how attractive the prospect of a rail journey may have been, a majority of *AOE* and now GrandLuxe passengers are, in fact, not familiar with rail travel and often carry on board with them expectations based on cruise ships. Once they've become acclimated, hung and stowed their clothes, and found a waiting glass of champagne at the Welcome Aboard reception in the *New York* observation or the *Seattle* or *Rocky Mountain* lounge, things begin to look much better—particularly for those patrons in suites (and, as GrandLuxe moves ahead with renovations, that will be virtually everyone).

Then, as the train begins to move, the true magic begins. The kaleidoscope of scenes starts to spin. The cars come alive with the excitement of motion, and with the rumble of steel wheels on steel rail. And then it's dinnertime. Perhaps there's an invitation to dine in the dome, which comes once a trip for everyone. Otherwise, the wood-paneled elegance of *Chicago* or *Zurich* is a worthy setting for a fine multi-course dinner.

That "AOE" stands for "another opportunity to eat" was a jocular staple of the tour leaders' pre-trip orientation. ("Good luck reducing" was quickly suggested by one tour leader for "GLR.") As on cruise ships, which the train in many ways emulates, food is plentiful: three squares in the diners (or lavish luncheons off the train on long tours), Continental breakfast and light lunch in the lounges as an alternative, hors d'oeuvres at cocktail hour, snacks on the bus. Still, the emphasis is firmly on quality rather than quantity. Portions are consciously sized so a dinner of appetizer, soup, salad, entrée, and dessert is not too much of a good thing.

The food has always been good on *AOE*, but when in 1999 the company hired Anthony Hubbard, an exciting young chef who graduated from the Johnson and Wales Culinary Institute in Rhode Island, cuisine was set on its current course of excellence. Previously, Hubbard had cooked in some outstanding Seattle restaurants and served as sous-chef aboard the *AOE*.

His five-course dinners were spectacular, with a choice from among five entrees. One set of options: beef tenderloin with green peppercorn brandy sauce, basil-encrusted salmon with lemon dill sauce, roasted chicken breast with olive tapenade, kasu-marinated sea bass with miso vinaigrette, or seared breast of duck with citrus ginger sauce. Desserts were no less impressive, and all the courses looked as good as they tasted.

"A perfect mix of art and chemistry," Hubbard called his work in *Zurich*'s and *Chicago*'s compact kitchens. There his able staff (including the pastry chef, Daniela Cole, who had trained at the Culinary Institute of America in Hyde Park, New York, and would eventually take over the kitchen from him), working with his personal recipes, turned out a succession of fine, fresh fare. Hubbard understood the importance of food to the train's success.

"There are many things about this operation that are beyond our control," he said. Classic but elderly equipment can break down, tracks can be rough, the weather can be bad, and the operating railroads can deliver the train late.

"But," Hubbard concluded, "the quality and presentation of meals is one thing we can control, so it's important that they are consistently excellent." Since Hubbard's departure, worthy successors have replaced him in the kitchen, beginning with Cole. Warren McLeod, a former marine, was a mainstay for three seasons, and Jeffrey Martin took over in 2005.

The patterns and pleasures of life on board have evolved through the years, without changing radically. Attentive service from the sleeping-car porter has been the norm. (*AOE* retained that traditional title, but GrandLuxe in 2007 split car-attendant duties between a "porter" and a "butler" team covering two sleepers.) He or she will "make down" your bed, reserve a shower time (for passengers in Vintage Pullmans or singles), and knock on the door (with coffee, tea, or orange juice, if requested) at the desired time. Service in the two dining cars is open seating, with dinner typically running from 6:00 to 9:00 PM.

The pleasures of a *GrandLuxe Express* journey is an amalgam of what goes on off the train—the tours, typically to historic sites and our great national parks—and on board. Pleasures of the on-train experience, in addition to meals, include music in the piano lounge before and after dinner, lectures in the dome, and, perhaps most important of all, getting to know fellow passengers. Certainly some lasting friendships have been born in the diners and lounges of the *AOE* and *GLR*. (One of the dubious amenities never available on *AOE* was television or video of any kind.)

For some passengers, more important than tours and meals and friendships is where the train goes, with an obvious consideration being scenery, and certainly the train does traverse some of the most beautiful country in North America. On and off and happily now on again is the former Denver & Rio Grande Western (currently Union Pacific) route across Colorado: the sweeping, looping ascent of the Front Range of the Rockies, and the 238 miles paralleling the Colorado River that takes the train through Byers, Gore, Red, Glenwood, and Ruby canyons. The passage through the Sierras and over Donner Pass on that same "Rockies & Sierras" itinerary is fine as well, and the Canadian Rockies near Jasper and to the west are no less spectacular when seen from Canadian National's line, which GrandLuxe plans to feature again in the future. Another highlight, on the "Great Northwest & Rockies" trip, is the run on BNSF Railway's ex–Great Northern line along Glacier National Park's southern boundary. (Glacier and Grand Canyon are two of only three great western parks with direct rail access, and in both cases *GrandLuxe Express* takes good advantage. And it's not out of the question that it may someday soon serve the third park, Alaska's Denali.)

For a certain small subset of travelers, however, scenery is not the primary attraction of certain routes. These customers are the "rare mileage" collectors, whose aim is to highlight in their rail atlases as many routes as possible. Their goal is to travel over lines that don't regularly see passenger trains, and the *GrandLuxe Express* (and *AOE* before it) is often just the ticket. Both scenic and rare, the "Great Northwest & Rockies" run over Montana Rail Link includes many miles along the Clark Fork River and over Mullan Pass, tiptoeing across a pair of towering curved trestles to reach it. Both that itinerary and "National Parks of the West" bump along the UP line that, until Amtrak arrived in 1971, hosted the *Butte Special,* but nothing since.

Other rare mileage has come and gone, such as the ex–Western Pacific (now UP) Feather River Canyon line, and the ex–WP-Great Northern "Inside Gateway" (now BNSF) that connects with it at Keddie, California. These routes were part of the "Pacific Coast Explorer" itinerary for a number of years. The run the "Parks" trips used to make up (and will again in 2008) the branch to Cedar City, Utah, built by UP to serve Zion and Bryce national parks, certainly qualified—and, because there were no turning facilities at the end, the train had to back the branch's 23-mile length, giving engineer's-eye views to passengers in *New York.* Some "Parks" trips jounced up the Santa Fe Southern line right into Santa Fe, rather than bussing passengers there from Albuquerque. Since short-line Santa Fe Southern operates a mixed train to accommodate excursionists, this doesn't qualify as true "rare mileage" but was a special treat for mileage hounds nonetheless. The same might be said of the run to the South Rim of the Grand Canyon on the Grand Canyon Railway, also a staple of the "Parks" itinerary.

As operated in 2003 and 2004, "Autumn in New England & Quebec" covered some rare mileage, a scenic stretch of the Green Mountain Railroad from Whitehall, New York, to Bellows Falls, Vermont. The Canadian Pacific (former Delaware & Hudson) route along Lake Champlain and New England Central's former Central Vermont route were included, too; not rare, since Amtrak trains travel them, though they were certainly scenic. And among the mileage buffs' greatest coups was a segment of the Canadian transcontinental itinerary, the Canadian National line between Thunder Bay, Ontario, and Winnipeg, Manitoba, included to get the train to Thunder Bay for touring there. Long without a regular passenger train, this route swerves briefly into Minnesota to skirt the southern shore of Lake of the Woods. (Those passengers not seeking rare mileage were less than thrilled by the two customs delays and the sealing off of liquor supplies for the short passage through the United States that this route entailed.)

Another somewhat obscure source of passenger pleasure could be the train's parking venue when stationary. Some locations, like Portland's handsomely restored Union Station, a fine Italian Renaissance–style structure opened in 1896, was a particularly rewarding place to be "stabled" (often so-called by staff, rather than "parked," presumably making a connection with the term "iron horse") on "Pacific Coast Explorer" trips. So, in a very different way, was the evening spent parked on a siding right on the shores of the Pacific Ocean at Paso Robles, California,

on the same itinerary. More often than not, however, the train had to be spotted overnight anyplace that was secure and could accommodate its length, an increasingly thorny issue as the consist grew.

Each passenger finds the particular pleasures that suit. Food, drink, music, naps, books, card games, scenery, sightseeing, photography, train-watching, learning, loafing—all of these can be more fun on a train than elsewhere. And, in North America at least, as pianist John Wallowitch wrote and sang way back when it all began, "No train compares with this show train."

Executive Chef Anthony Hubbard. *Karl Zimmermann.*

AMERICAN ORIENT EXPRESS

ROCKIES & SIERRAS
WEDNESDAY
OCTOBER 19th, 2005

EN ROUTE TO GRAND JUNCTION, CO

<u>Appetizer</u>

Cajun Rock Shrimp
served with Brandy Cream

<u>Soup</u>

Potato Leek
garnished with Chives

<u>Salad</u>

Classic Caesar
Romaine tossed in Caesar dressing, topped with
Garlic Croutons, and fresh Parmesan Cheese

LUXURY   PRIVATE   TRAIN

Dinner menus.
Karl Zimmermann Collection.

AMERICAN ORIENT EXPRESS

<u>Entrees</u>

Slow Roasted Prime Rib
served with Horseradish mashed Potatoes, creamed
Spinach, and Rosemary Au Jus

****
Oven Roasted Rack of Lamb
accompanied by Turmeric infused Polenta, baby Patty
Pan Squash, and drizzled with Pomegranate Molasses

****
Lobster and Goat Cheese Stuffed Halibut
served on a bed of steamed Jasmine Rice with
sautéed Tri-color Peppers, and Lemon Beurre Blanc

Half portions are available

<u>Desserts</u>

Dark Chocolate Raspberry Cheesecake
garnished with Raspberry Coulis and fresh Berries

****
Bananas Foster
Bananas in a Rum Carmel sauce served over
Vanilla Ice Cream

****
Seasonal Fresh Fruit

Executive Chef Courtney Nguyen
Pastry Chef Elisa Hindes

LUXURY   PRIVATE   TRAIN

Along the Thompson River, Vancouver-bound.
Karl Zimmermann.

Along the Connecticut River near Bellow Falls, Vermont,
September 30, 2003. *Jim Shaughnessy.*

At Riverside, Vermont, on the Green Mountain Railroad in
late October 2004. *Jim Shaughnessy.*

At the depot in Santa Fe in October 1998. *Karl Zimmermann.*

BELOW: The *AOE* and the Grand Canyon Railway excursion meet at Imbleau, Arizona, on May 30, 2004. *Steve Patterson.*

The *AOE* overnights in Portland. *Karl Zimmermann.*

ABOVE: Rolling across Texas at dawn on "The Great Transcontinental Rail Journey." *Karl Zimmermann.*

In Jasper, passengers return to the *AOE* in light rain. *Karl Zimmermann.*

Appendix: all-time roster of cars operated by the American Orient Express

AOE Name	Car	Manufacturer, Year Built	Year of Lease
American Spirit	Dome lounge (GN dome chair car #1325 for *Empire Builder*)	Budd, 1955	2004 season
Bar Harbor	7–Grand Suite, 1–Single Room sleeper (UP 44-seat chair car #5539)	SLC, 1964	
*Berlin**	2–Presidential Suite (Harry S. Truman, Woodrow Wilson), 7–Vintage Pullman sleeper (UP—11–double bedroom *Placid Lake*)	P-S, 1956	
Charleston	7–Grand Suite, 1–Single Room sleeper (UP 44-seat chair car #5494)	SLC, 1960	
*Chicago**	42-seat diner (UP lunch counter diner-lounge #5014)	SLC, 1959	
*Cimarron River***	Crew sleeper (SLSF 12-roomette, 4–double bedroom sleeper for *Meteor*)	P-S, 1948	1996 season
*Colorado River***	Crew sleeper (FEC 10-roomette, 6–double bedroom *Argentina*)	P-S, 1949	2003 season
*Columbia River***	Dome diner (UP dome diner #8009 for *City of Portland*)	ACF, 1955	1997 season
Copper Canyon	Dome-lounge (CB&Q "Great Dome" *River View* for *Empire Builder*)	Budd, 1955	
Denver	7–Grand Suite, 1–Single Room sleeper (UP 44-seat chair car #5490)	SLC, 1960	
*Glacier Park***	Dome observation lounge (UP dome lounge observation #9007 for *City of Portland*)	ACF, 1955	2003 season
Grand Canyon	Crew sleeper (UP—11–double bedroom sleeper *Placid Scene*)	P-S, 1956	
*Istanbul**	2–Presidential Suite (William Henry Harrison, William McKinley), 2–Parlor Suite (Charles Crocker, Mark Hopkins), 4 Vintage Pullman sleeper (SP 4-compartment, 4–double bedroom, 2–drawing room sleeper #9119 for *Cascade*)	P-S, 1950	
Jasper	Dining-room car (with *Vancouver*, UP twin-unit dormitory-kitchen/dining room–waiting lounge #5106 for *City of Denver*); renumbered 5113	ACF, 1953	2002–2004 seasons
Los Angeles	Laundry car (SP baggage dormitory #3103 for *Sunset Limited*)	Budd, 1950	
*Monte Carlo**	2–Presidential Suite (Thomas Jefferson, Grover Cleveland), 8–Vintage Pullman sleeper (B&O 10-roomette, 6–double bedroom sleeper *Opequon*)	P-S, 1950	
*Monterey***	Crew sleeper/diner (C&O 5-bedroom buffet-lounge observation *Wolverine Club*; to B&O as *Wawasee* in 1951 for *Capital Limited*)	P-S, 1950	7-year lease, then purchase

AOE Name	Car	Manufacturer, Year Built	Year of Lease
Montreal	3–Presidential Suite (Martin Van Buren, Lyndon Baines Johnson, George Washington), 5–Vintage Pullman sleeper (UP 5–double bedroom buffet lounge *North Platte*; rebuilt 1965 as 11–double bedroom *Star Scene*)	P-S, 1956	
New Orleans	Dome-lounge (GN "Great Dome" *Mountain View* for *Empire Builder*)	Budd, 1955	
New York*	Observation car (NYC *Sandy Creek*, 5–double bedroom buffet-observation for *20th Century Limited*)	P-S, 1948	
Northern Sky**	Dome-lounge sleeper (UP dome lounge observation #9003 for *City of Los Angeles*)	ACF, 1955	1996 season
Pacific Star	Crew sleeper (UP 5–double bedroom buffet lounge *La Grande*; rebuilt 1965 as 11–double bedroom *Star Range*)	P-S, 1956	
Paris*	2–Presidential Suite (Andrew Jackson, John Quincy Adams), 2 Parlor Suite (Collis P. Huntington, Leland Stanford), 4–Vintage Pullman sleeper (SP 4-compartment, 4–double bedroom, 2–drawing room sleeper #9120 for *Cascade*)	P-S, 1950	
Portland**	Sleeper (*Bella Vista*, C&O *Homestead*, 11–double bedroom sleeper)	P-S, 1950	7-year lease, then purchase
Rocky Mountain*	Club car (UP *Alpine View*, 14-section sleeper; converted to 44-seat coach 1965, named *St. Moritz* in *AEE* service)	ACF, 1954	
San Antonio	Laundry/baggage/shop car (Army ambulance car #USAX 89523)	SLC, 1953	
San Francisco**	Sleeper/crew diner (*Montecito*, NKP 5–double bedroom café-lounge *City of Cleveland*)	P-S, 1950	7-year lease, then purchase
Santa Fe	3–Presidential Suite (Franklin Delano Roosevelt, Abraham Lincoln, John F. Kennedy), 5–Vintage Pullman sleeper (UP 5–double bedroom buffet lounge *Cheyenne*; rebuilt 1965 as 11–double bedroom *Star Crest*)	P-S, 1956	
Savannah	7–Grand Suite, 1–Single Room sleeper (UP 44-seat chair car #5500)	SLC, 1960	
Seattle*	Club car (UP 14-section sleeper *Alpine Meadow*; converted to 44-seat coach 1965, named *Bay Point Club* in *AEE* service)	ACF, 1954	
Silver Solarium**	Dome-observation lounge (CB&Q 1–drawing room, 3–double bedroom dome-observation lounge for *California Zephyr*)	Budd, 1948	2002 season
Swift Stream	Crew sleeper/diner (NYC 6–double bedroom buffet lounge)	Budd, 1949	2002 season
Tallahassee	Crew sleeper (SAL 11–double bedroom sleeper)	P-S, 1956	
Vancouver	Galley Car (with Jasper, UP twin-unit dormitory-kitchen dining room–waiting lounge #5106 for *City of Denver*); renumbered 5112	ACF, 1953	2002–2004 seasons

AOE Name	Car	Manufacturer, Year Built	Year of Lease
Vienna*	2–Presidential Suite (Henry L. Hillman, Dwight D. Eisenhower), 7–Vintage Pullman sleeper (UP 11–double bedroom *Placid Waters*)	P-S, 1956	
Washington*	2–Presidential Suite (William Howard Taft, Theodore Roosevelt), 8–Vintage Pullman sleeper (C&O 10-roomette, 6–double bedroom sleeper *City of Staunton*)	P-S, 1950	
Yellowstone Park	Crew sleeper (CB&Q 6–double bedroom 5-compartment sleeper *Silver Pelican* for *Denver Zephyr*)	Budd, 1956	
Zurich*	46-seat diner (UP café-lounge #5004; rebuilt by UP as lunch-counter diner-lounge)	ACF, 1949	

* = former *American-European Express* car

** = leased

Sleeping-car configurations and suite names are accurate as of the cars' conveyance from *American Orient Express* to GrandLuxe Rail Journeys. GLR made some changes for the 2007 season and no doubt will make more.

Abbreviations

Builders:
ACF = American Car & Foundry
Budd = The Budd Company
P-S = Pullman-Standard
SLC = St. Louis Car Company

Railroads:
AR = Alaska Railroad
B&O = Baltimore & Ohio Railroad
C&O = Chesapeake & Ohio Railway
CB&Q = Chicago, Burlington & Quincy Railroad
FEC = Florida East Coast Railway

GN = Great Northern Railway
IC = Illinois Central Railroad
NKP = Nickel Plate Road (New York, Chicago & St. Louis Railroad)
NYC = New York Central Railroad
SAL = Seaboard Air Line
SLSF = Frisco (St. Louis & San Francisco)
SP = Southern Pacific Lines
UP = Union Pacific Railroad

BIBLIOGRAPHY

Books

Dubin, Arthur. *Some Classic Trains*. Milwaukee: Kalmbach, 1964.

Hogg, Gary. *Orient Express: The Birth, Life, and Death of a Great Train*. New York: Walker and Co., 1968.

Morgan, Bryan, ed. *The Great Trains*. New York: Crown, 1973.

Sherwood, Shirley. *Venice Simplon Orient-Express: The Return of the World's Most Celebrated Train*. London: Weidenfeld and Nicolson, 1983.

Wayner, Robert J. *Car Names, Numbers and Consists*. New York: Wayner, 1972.

Zimmermann, Karl R. *CZ: The Story of the California Zephyr*. Starrucca, Pa.: Starrucca Valley, 1972.

———. *Santa Fe Streamliners: The Chiefs and Their Tribesmen*. New York: Quadrant, 1987.

Articles

"Bowing to Troubles, Luxury Train Ends Service." *The New York Times* (October 22, 1991).

Johnston, Bob. "Luxury Rail Cruising at a Crossroads." *Passenger Train Journal* XXII (March 1991): 20–29.

Wagner, Ralcon. "Neiman Marcus Takes to the Rails." *Trains* LVI (March 1996): 30.

Books in the Railroads Past and Present Series

Landmarks on the Iron Railroad: Two Centuries of North American Railroad Engineering by William D. Middleton

South Shore: The Last Interurban (revised second edition) by William D. Middleton

"Yet there isn't a train I wouldn't take": Railroad Journeys by William D. Middleton

The Pennsylvania Railroad in Indiana by William J. Watt

In the Traces: Railroad Paintings of Ted Rose by Ted Rose

A Sampling of Penn Central: Southern Region on Display by Jerry Taylor

The Lake Shore Electric Railway by Herbert H. Harwood, Jr., and Robert S. Korach

The Pennsylvania Railroad at Bay: William Riley McKeen and the Terre Haute and Indianapolis Railroad by Richard T. Wallis

The Bridge at Quebec by William D. Middleton

History of the J. G. Brill Company by Debra Brill

When the Steam Railroads Electrified by William D. Middleton

Uncle Sam's Locomotives: The USRA and the Nation's Railroads by Eugene L. Huddleston

Metropolitan Railways: Rapid Transit in America by William D. Middleton

Limiteds, Locals, and Expresses in Indiana, 1838–1971 by Craig Sanders

Perfecting the American Steam Locomotive by J. Parker Lamb

From Small Town to Downtown: A History of the Jewett Car Company, 1893–1919 by Lawrence A. Brough and James H. Graebner

Steel Trails of Hawkeyeland: Iowa's Railroad Experience by Don L. Hofsommer

Still Standing: A Century of Urban Train Station Design by Christopher Brown

The Indiana Rail Road Company: America's New Regional Railroad by Christopher Rund

Amtrak in the Heartland by Craig Sanders

The Men Who Loved Trains: The Story of Men Who Battled Greed to Save an Ailing Industry by Rush Loving Jr.

The Train Of Tomorrow by Ric Morgan

Evolution of the American Diesel Locomotive by J. Parker Lamb

The Encyclopedia of North American Railroads edited by William D. Middleton, George M. Smerk, and Roberta L. Diehl

KARL ZIMMERMANN is the author or co-author of 20 previous books, including *CZ: The Story of the California Zephyr; Santa Fe Streamliners: The Chiefs and Their Tribesmen;* and *Magnetic North: Canadian Steam in Twilight,* written with Roger Cook. An accomplished writer and photographer whose love of trains has sparked a lifetime of travel worldwide, Zimmermann has been a frequent contributor to the travel sections of newspapers across the country, including the *New York Times, Los Angeles Times,* and the *Washington Post.* His stories and photographs have appeared in *Trains, Classic Trains, Railfan & Railroad, Locomotive & Railway Preservation, Travel & Leisure, Gourmet, Outdoor Life,* and other magazines. Zimmermann is the North American Intercity columnist for *Passenger Train Journal* and a contributing editor to *The International Railway Traveler.*

ACQUIRING EDITOR: *Linda Oblack*
MANAGING EDITOR: *Miki Bird*
BOOK & JACKET DESIGN: *Pamela Rude*
COMPOSITION: *Pamela Rude & Tony Brewer*